OSVALDO ROMBERG
+/− 70, EVEN

OSVALDO ROMBERG
+/- 70, EVEN

Edited by Damien Bright and Cameron Hu

Contributions by:
Diana Franssen, Lorand Hegyi,
Robert Mahoney, Marcelin Pleynet,
Jean-Michel Rabaté and Hennie Westbrook

BARRYTOWN
STATION HILL

Barrytown/Station Hill Press
120 Station Hill Road Barrytown, New York 12507
www.stationhill.org

This publication has been produced in association with the Museo de Arte Moderno Buenos Aires.

We gratefully acknowledge that Barrytown/Station Hill Press and the Institute for Publishing Arts, Inc., a not-for-profit, Federally tax-exempt organization in Barrytown, New York, are funded in part by grants from The New York State Council on the Arts, a state agency.

Certain articles have appeared in the following publications acknowledged here:

Osvaldo Romberg. Bypass 1972-1997.
Kunstmuseum, Bonn, 1997

Searching for Romberg. Aaron Levy (Ed.)
Slought Books, Philadelphia, 2001

Osvaldo Romberg. Architectures Narratives/Narrative Architectures.
Editions du Panama, Paris, 2005.

Osvaldo Romberg. The Library is Burning. Text, Image, Object: 1963-2005.
Joint Stedelijk Van Abbemuseum, Eindhoven and University of Pennsylvania Library, Philadelphia, Exhibition Catalogue, 2005.

Translocations: Architectural Installations.
PeKA Gallery for Experimental Art and Architecture, Technion, Haifa, Exhibition Catalogue, 2005.

Designed by borborygmus (http://www.borborygmus.net/)

Library of Congress Cataloging-in-Publication Data

Osvaldo Romberg +/- 70, even / edited by Damien Bright & Cameron Hu.
    p. cm.
Includes texts by and about the artist, interviews, and the photographic survey of his work.
ISBN 978-1-58177-108-4 (alk. paper)
1. Romberg, Osvaldo, 1938- I. Bright, Damien, 1986- II. Hu, Cameron, 1986- III. Romberg, Osvaldo, 1938- IV. Title: Osvaldo Romberg plus/minus seventy, even.

N6639.R64O88 2008
709.2--dc22

                    2008014387

Printed in the U.S.A.

*"When I look at a work, and I don't know
how to eat it: maybe this is art."*
Osvaldo Romberg

CONTENTS

CONTENTS

This book began in Philadelphia in early 2007 and since then it has traveled across the American West Coast and into its Deep South, to France, Morocco, Syria and South Korea via Australia.

Osvaldo Romberg is both figure and ground, the subject of this text but also the range of signs through which it learned to speak. We struggled with that voice: we tried to overpower it with a chorus of others, we fabricated doubles, collaborators, opposing agents and a series of fictions. We cut pages out of catalogues and rearranged them, trying to impose ourselves on them with old collages and new classifications. We unearthed uncommodified materials both out of faithfulness to O.R's past and a desire to mine his present. Yet despite all these cut ups, or perhaps in spite of them, that voice is nonetheless stridently apparent.

We had therefore to ask ourselves who speaks through Osvaldo Romberg. Is it Jesus, Caravaggio, or Melnikov? Is it the mother, the sisters and the great controller? Is it Argentina, Israel, the Continent or the New World? Is it us, the spectators, first and last? These are not simply rhetorical questions, they call up three indissociable elements for the reading of Osvaldo Romberg's work: the successions of intellectual histories, the import of a personal biogeography and the retroactivity of audiences. As such, we decided it was not so important to speak about Osvaldo Romberg as it was to assemble each of these elements in its integrity.

To that extent, the images on the opposing pages provide the appropriate introduction to this project and Osvaldo Romberg himself. They are early slides,

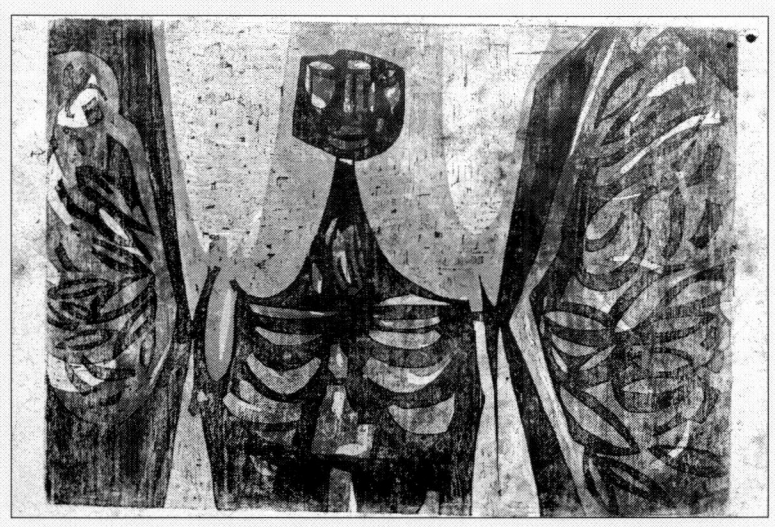

The Angel of Testimony. Color woodcut. 150 x 110 cm, 1961

previously unpublished documents from an artistic career that predates his now well-known reconstructions of visual space.

This project is not only the meeting of voices and a crossing of paths, it has also been a collaboration. We thank the artist's team of collaborators at his Philadelphia studio, particularly Didier and Susan, for guiding us through Romberg's archive. We are also grateful to Emmy de Martelaere, Aaron Levy and Giora Rozen for their insightful editorial recommendations. Thanks must also go to Tasha Doremus, Robin McDowell, Titus Nemeth and Aaron Shapiro for their contributions to this project. In addition, this book owes much to the assistance and faith of George and Susan Quasha, Jenny Fox and Station Hill Press. It has been a pleasure to work with them. And finally, of course, we wish to thank Osvaldo Romberg for his hospitality, for encouraging this exchange of art to art, of life to life.

We hope you enjoy what follows.

Damien Bright and Cameron Hu
Paris, 2009

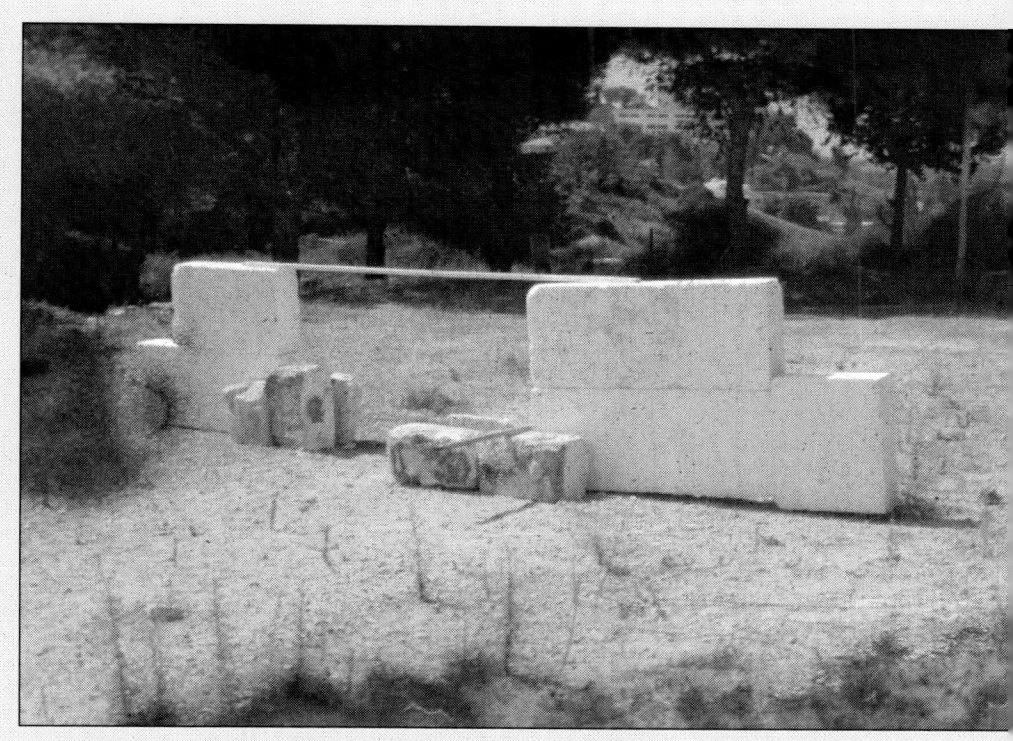

Sculpture with rocks and stones on landscape. Israel, 1973.

*I*t seems appropriate to begin with painting because painting is where it all started. Prehistoric paintings of animals on cave walls drew and blended the natureculture divide like two colors on a painter's palette, discrete at their centers though compromised on their borders. I first saw Osvaldo, a four-year old, repeating the gestures of his antecedents with pulp and pigment. The whiskers of a cat turned masterpiece, crudely, gingerly, reproduced by the child on wood purchased at the market by the father. The naïve and uncalculated irreverence that no integrated or acclimatised or accultured artist could afford. And yet six hours later, the copy lay complete in the artist's hands: a palimpsest of a culture past, a creation present, and a body of work to come.

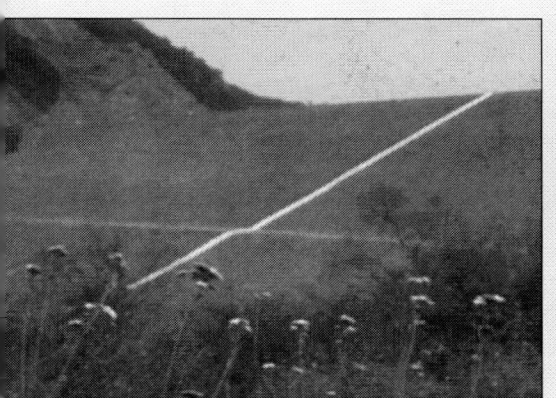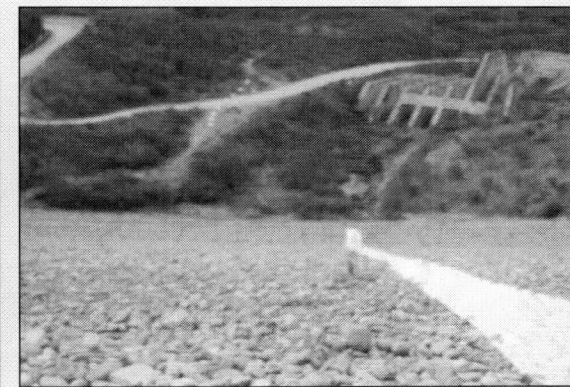

Two landscape interventions at Tucuman Landscape, 1969.

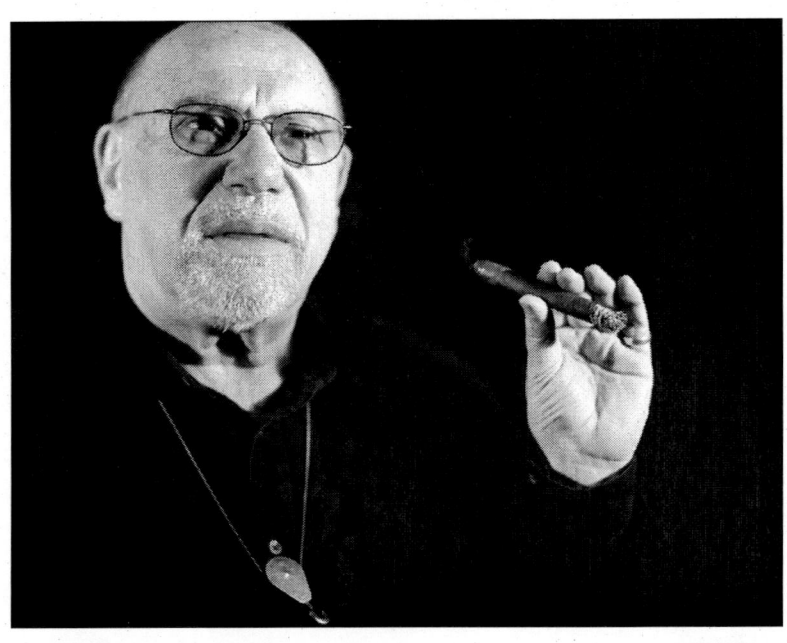

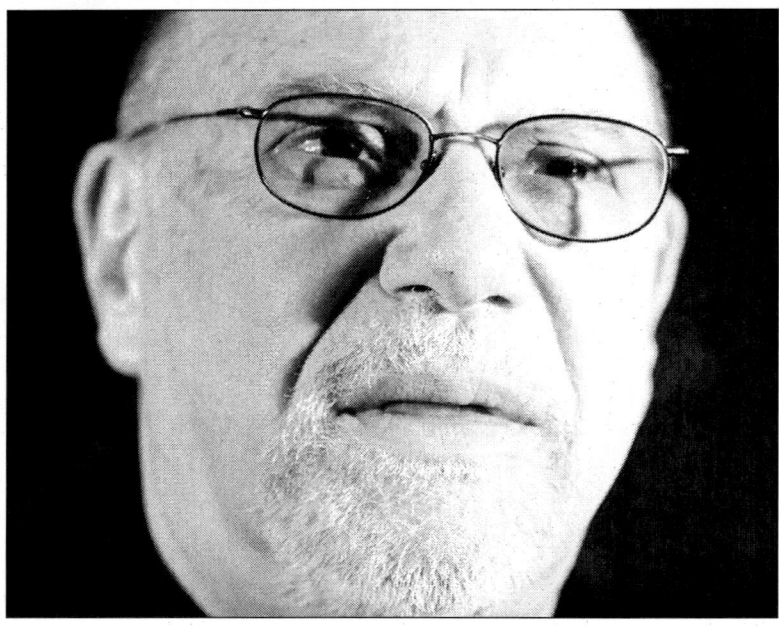

ABOUT
PAINTING

Years passed. My body translocated, – Sao Paolo, Beirut, London, Berlin – became experienced and bespoke experience in turn. Though trains and planes grew weary, I would lead the charge. Pages would turn at my quick fingers, buildings revealed themselves to my probing gaze, and cities opened

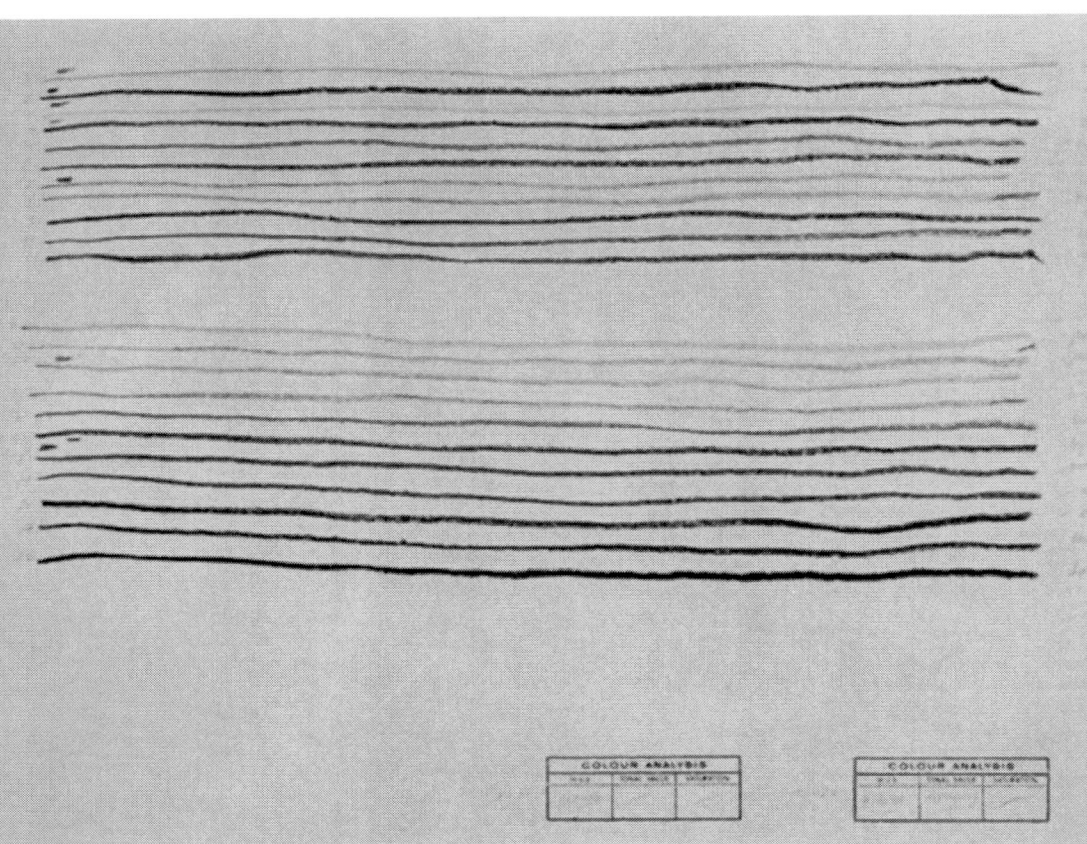

stupid like a painter
OSVALDO ROMBERG

THE GOOD PAINTER

Being an Argentinean adolescent artist was not easy. As soon as I began to interact with the artistic milieu in Buenos Aires in the 50s I submitted, with obsessive frequency, to the sentence: "But he's a good painter." From about 12 to 20 years of age, I desperately tried to understand, in the cafes and bars where we used to meet, the meaning of being a good painter. The different answers were concerned at times with the quality of the textures on the canvas, at other times with the construction and the form of the figure, the flatness, or even the purity of the pigment. I had only decontextualized particulars available to me, fragments of different discourses. How right Duchamp was in his commentary on the I.Q. of painters, when he proposed the phrase "Stupid like a

I do not know very much about my origins. I only knew my Grandfather and my Grandmother, who were from Russia. They told me stories when I was young, of which I remember very little. He ran away from the Russian and Japanese war to Argentina; my father, who was four years old, came with him.

up to the sound of my impatient feet. An avid diarist, my movements — gesturing hands and impatient feet — transcribed themselves in space, like lines in a ledger. Yet East and West were not targets mapped onto a compass, but pulls and shifts felt [bodily] as I waded through Ahab's wake. There was no center to

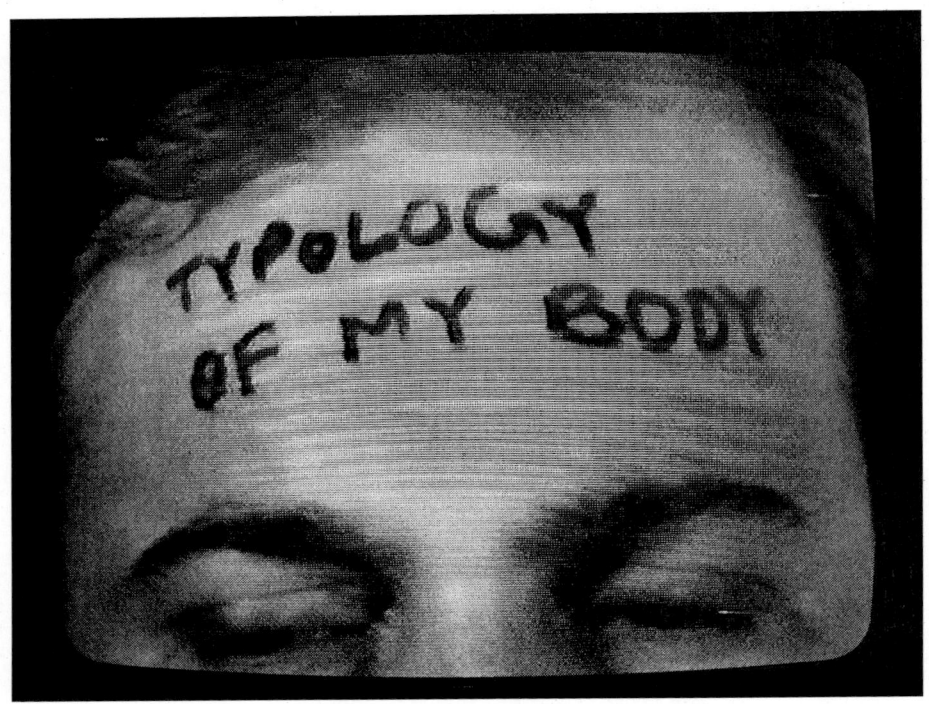

painter." (We should not forget that the 50s were particularly difficult, at least in Argentina, for those who wished to talk abut artists as a category because there were painters, sculptors, draftsmen, etc. The concept of an artist who thinks and directs his ideas visually was simply not common in Buenos Aires then).

Tragically, these peripheral phenomena that I saw in Argentina are much too frequently observed in the galleries of New York today. Of the few artists who are definitely "hot" (meaning being in fashion because of prestige or for evidencing astonishing innovation, opportunism, gender promotion or other means of self-legitimization), most of the galleries (even the prestigious ones) put their bets on "good painters" – who of course will have the upper class, kitschy marketability desired by the majority of American collectors. Here is where the work or the practice of Marjorie Welish comes to light and shines for us in a scenario desperately in need of illumination.

THE GOOD LIE

When looking at the history of art from the last two centuries, it is easy to observe that as soon as your subject matter departs from nature, you need to replace the theory of duplication with a theory that legitimizes your lack of reality in representation. The further away from the original model of nature (in which you aim for the reproduction of what you see), the more complex and sophisticated your story should be. This is obviously evident from Impressionism to the contemporary period. And I will say that passing through Fauvism, Cubism, and Surrealism, the process of explanation becomes more subjective and complex. When we arrive at Abstraction, the road of self-referential painting that Cézanne put forward ends majestically with Mondrian referring to the borders of the picture.

From now on, when talking about abstraction, we are nearly in the land of Clement Greenberg. Both the story justifying our lack of mimesis and the brilliant subjectivity required of us are more and more demanding. I will put it into a simple story: imagine somebody speeding in a car at 180 miles per hour who is stopped by a state trooper. The driver needs to find a very good "lie," For otherwise he will not be able to convince the police that he is not a transgressor. Here again, the work of Marjorie Welish comes to mind. I would say that Marjorie does not invent a good lie to justify her speeding car (her

grasp, nor periphery to displace. In the desert I came across two brothers, each building a city on two opposing plots. The first, let us call him José, had mapped a precise system of grids: he organized the city's different elements into discrete and categorized space. He believed that he would thereby serve the horizontal

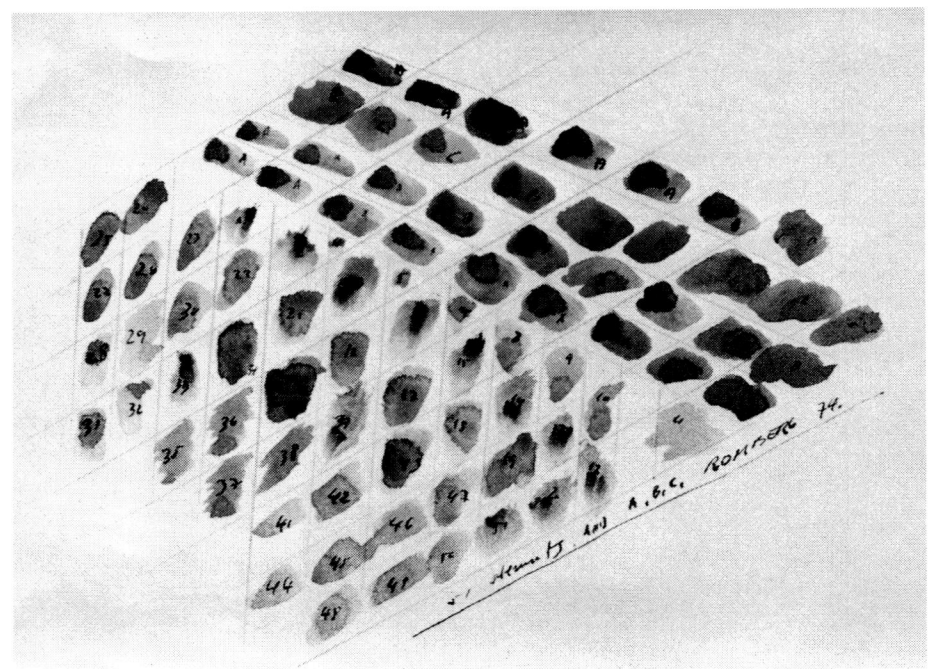

abstraction); rather, she is running at a far greater speed, onto an epistemological road (and quest) in which there are no police, no limits but the land of spirituality – nobody's land.

What makes the story of Marjorie different from that of Kenneth Noland, Morris Louis or any other artist who lives near the Greenberg cult is the following: her discourse, though humbly subjective, is specifically about painting and grammar. She is a kind of story teller, and her work is a kind of commentary on the difficulty of painting. Her work does not employ a tricky gag so as to conform to or belong to a school of abstraction. Nor does she put herself in the ridiculous position of many abstract artists today who pretend to save abstraction from its inevitable fate in decoration.

THE RETURN OF THE HORSE

Painting has almost become an aristocratic activity like riding horses, but this is not where the similarity ends. Let us remember that some centuries ago it was impossible to go from New York to Philadelphia without a good horse, just as it was impossible to show somebody's features without a good portrait painting.

Without doubt, the similarities do not

I was born in Buenos Aires in 1938 in the neighbourhood of Villa Crespo; it was a mixed Jewish and Catholic neighbourhood. My father was the community doctor, and the local primary school I attended had a very mixed population. I had two sisters, Chola and Regina, who were much older than me.

and vertical richness of life. His brother, let us call him Enrique, bemoaned the simplicity of José's system. He spoke of his own city, in which the wilderness would not be bridled, but manifest and apparent. And so the borders of Enrique's city shifted continuously, unreliably, much like the mood and make-up of

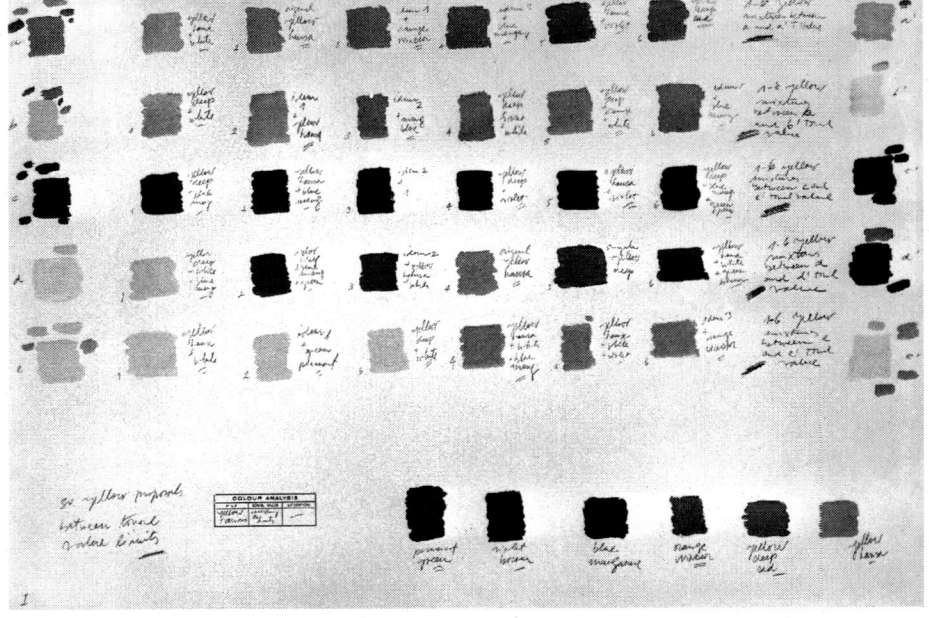

end here. Both underwent mutations, which made them in a way anachronistic to their original functions. Today, transportation is not reliant upon the horse, and contemporary art, in turn, has enormously reduced the activity of painting from the primary mode of expression — it is now a secondary, anachronistic form. If what was once transport is, today, almost a sport, the question remains if the function of the horse will return to transportation. Will painting become the central issue in contemporary art again? If so, when?

Questions appropriate to our debate: when does a special situation allow for the return of an old form of expression? Sometimes, a geographical situation like mountains with special terrain or a military strategy like that employed in Afghanistan requires horses. Thus, does the horse return to its original function, or is it replaced with artificial horses in specific situations. Does painting return to its original function or will it be replaced by video, holograms or other media?

Where is the future of painting? In this moment, it seems that unless it is "retro," the field of painting is reduced to commentary or paintings which try to explore the limited possibilities of the

Your father and mother always lie to you. One of the problems of the world is that we don't tell our children the truth. We hand them our superego. And that's the way they become screwed up.

its population. I try to imagine what would have happened, if his variegated city had been founded on an island. How would it take on water? What adjusting would it do within, what adjustments would it make without? When its limits

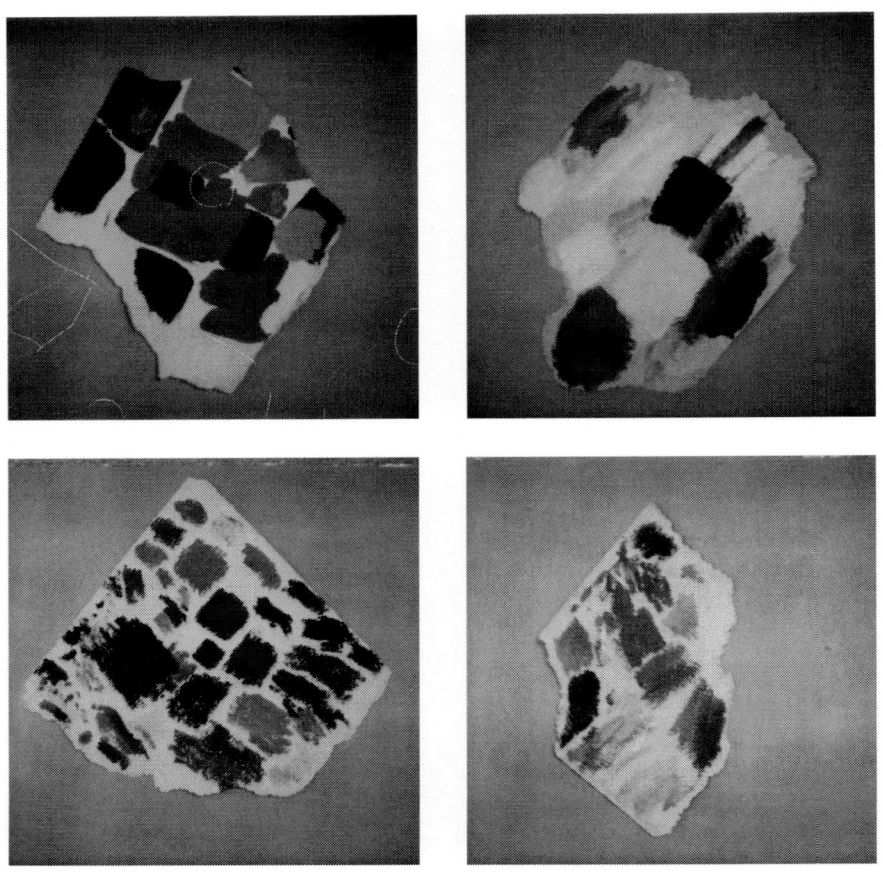

subject. What is it possible to do with painting that cannot be done with anything else? Here again we come to the work of Marjorie Welish, because her late work articulates with enormous insight the mechanics of Modernist painting in a manner impossible to describe in words.

In this sense, I feel myself to be an artist whose work of the 70s has an affinity with her work of today. The didactics of Marjorie's work is only pictorially expressive. It cannot be articulated in any written or oral explanation. (Maybe that is why I am joking so much today!). The work of art, in this case a painting, physically embodies its meaning. She creates a lot of empty space for viewers so that they can articulate their own discourse about what they see. As is the case in any other field of complex expression, the work of Marjorie Welish requires knowledge and sophistication. In her case, and against Greenberg's idea of the reduction of content, her work shows a very interesting thesis, namely, "the more you know the more you get."

In 1951, I was accepted into the best and most rigorous secondary school in Buenos Aires: the Colegio National de Buenos Aires. After that, I spent a few years studying architecture at the University of Buenos Aires. I never completed my studies there because I realised that I could never design for anyone other than myself.

28 | *seem so naturally immediate, how would such a city mediate [its] expression? Landlocked for a time, I took up the study of plants. From deciduous to ever-green, underbrush to canopies, I compiled a survey of Alberta, Minnesota. My*

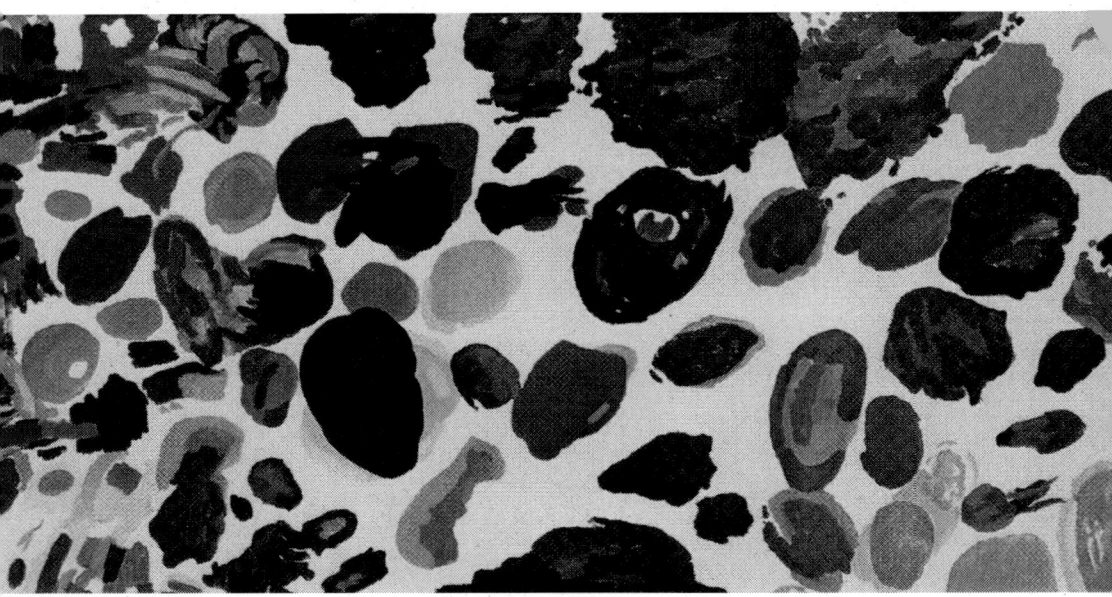

art to art. life to life.
OSVALDO ROMBERG

Art begins when life is not enough.

In modern culture the acceptance of death signifies the loss of connection with the infinite. It is in this the loss of the infinite, that art gives relief and new hopes for spirituality.

Art makes evident (and occasionally succeeds in resolving) the conflict between being and integrating with the world. This is a dilemma which religion can no longer address.

When Caravaggio humanized Christian icons by painting ordinary people, Velazquez and Rembrandt immediately reversed the trend, and re-aestheticized the world of god for Christianity.

All the religions of the world are narratives. In these narratives are implicit my-

My mother told me when I was four and I had an erection that if I touched my penis it would fall off. Imagine the influence that had on me.

My mother's father was an ebonist. He carved furniture, and he died when I was a child. A few years later, my maternal grandmother passed away as well. My mother was a very wonderful person, a very good person. She was not very cultivated, but had a fantastic naiveté about her.

collected samples numbered seeds, barks, leaves, roots, shoots, and buds, each identified by name and provenance. I returned to Alberta some years later. The scene was impressive, a vision of abundance and expansion; countless permuta-

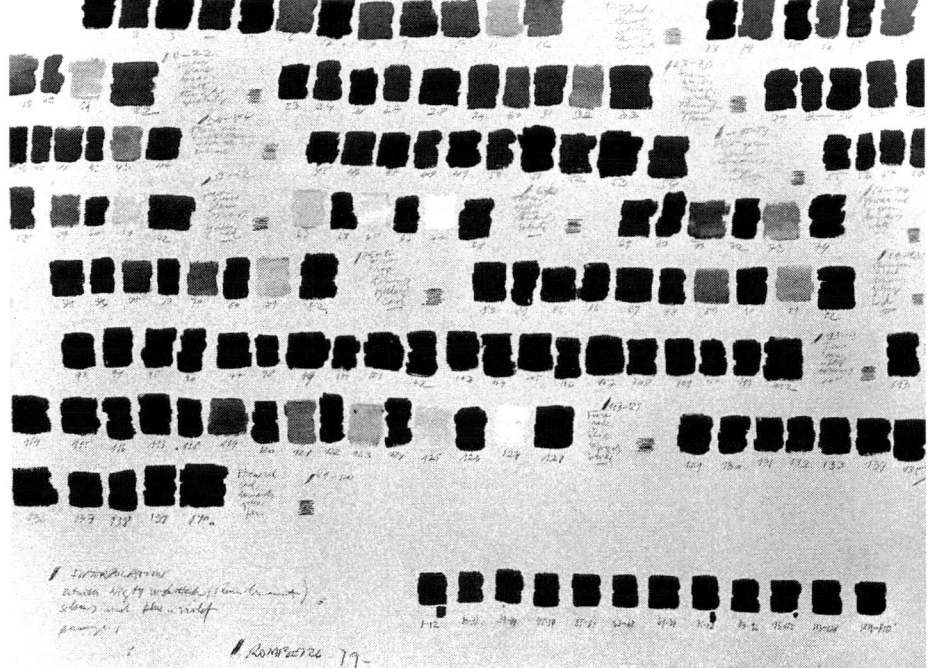

thologies and explanations which help people to survive the panic of death and solitude. In the past, art merely rearticulated these narratives. In recent years, however, I have observed that art is replacing religion by raising its own issues of morality, identity, mortality, and transcendence.

Art used to be the illustration of the metaphysical. It has now become the metaphysical itself. The vitality and dynamism of contemporary art challenges religions ability to face the relevant issues at the end of the millennium: artificiality, reproduction of the species, and equality.

The search for originality, so typical of the modern artist who claims to be unique, is shaped by our idea of God as creator. From nothing, God created matter and the organization of matter, which is life. The artist takes white canvas, organizes it, and creates meaning. It seems that the mission of the artist is to create meaning for others. Is that not a religious endeavor?

The metaphorical nature of art touches the spiritual while bypassing reason and intelligence. Art is where the organic and metaphysical meet in that unique place where pure signification can be found.

Paraphrasing Martin Heidegger, we can say that the authentic dialogue with the art of an artist is artistic, as opposed to critical. There is no artistic dialogue between artists and those who do not believe in the power of art to contain essential truths.

Heidegger showed and established after Johann Christian Friedrich Hölderlin that a poem (a work of art) replaces philosophy. He declared that philosophy is a prisoner of science (positivism) and politics (Marxism).

In a sense, conceptual art returns to Judaism as it eliminates the image and focuses on the word. The hermeneutic tendencies of modern art can also be related to the Jewish practice of Talmudic study, essentially to the everyday life of a Jew on every social level. For Jews, the answer is also a question.

For a true artist, the world of art is reality, and the world of reality is a corporeal fiction. That is why it is difficult for artists to function in both worlds. It is easier to gain understanding of the energy of the cosmos looking at Pollock than listening to a lecture by a scientist.

Marcel Duchamp, who did to representation what Friedrich Nietzche did to re-

tions and uncharted strains lay underfoot. I failed to get my head around them all; the samples I had mapped could not account for forms. Provenance was gone, taxonomy remained.

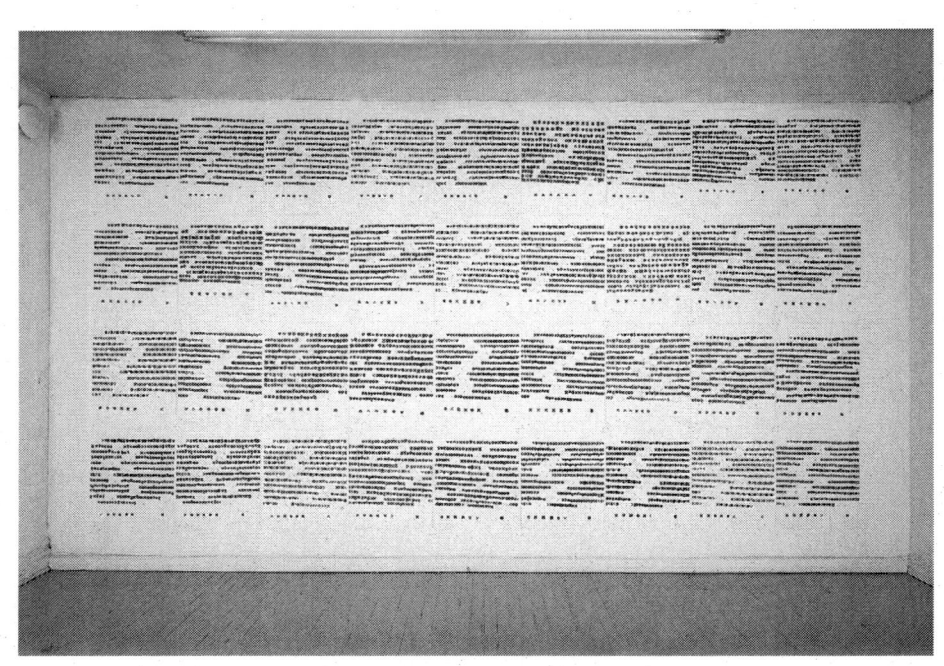

ligion, used the ready-made to "present,"
not to "represent." Johns and Rauschen-
berg, etc., are the "counter-reformers"
who collaged real objects into the rep-
resentational space of their paintings.

The idea of art as a regenerative activity
is described in *The Glass Bead Game* by
Hermann Hesse. The book is about the
translation of all information systems
and human knowledge into one code,
the Game. Once you enter this universal
language, you can integrate all aspects of
human experience. Marcel Duchamp is
the "Magister Ludi."

Referring to *The Bride Stripped Bare by
her Bachelors, Even* in a 1966 interview
with Pierre Cabanne, Duchamp said, "...I
almost never put any calculations into
the large Glass. Simply, I thought of the
idea of a projection, of an invisible fourth
dimension, something you couldn't see
with your eyes." Is this not the domain
of the divine?

*My mother was Russian but spoke with
me first in Spanish. I spoke French before
speaking English, maybe it was a cultural
affinity. Even today, despite living in America
for all these years, I think I speak better
French than English.*

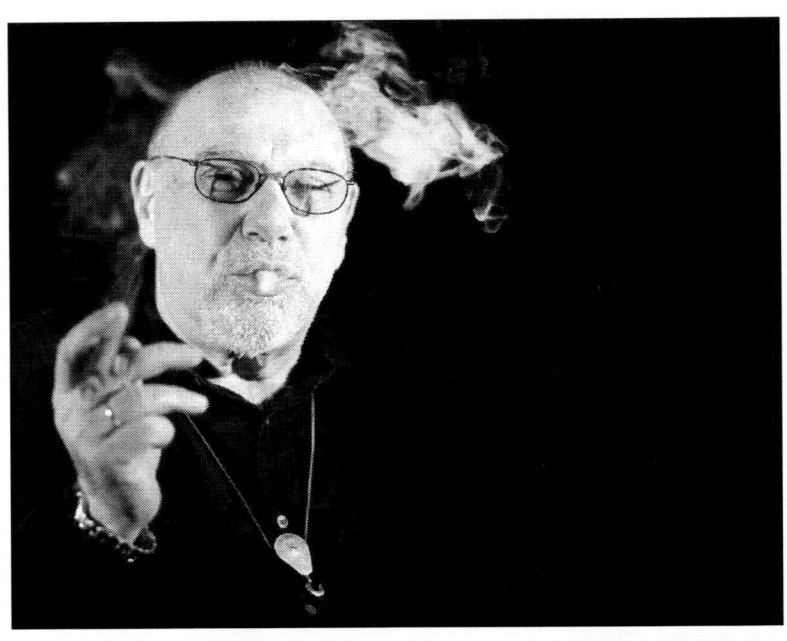
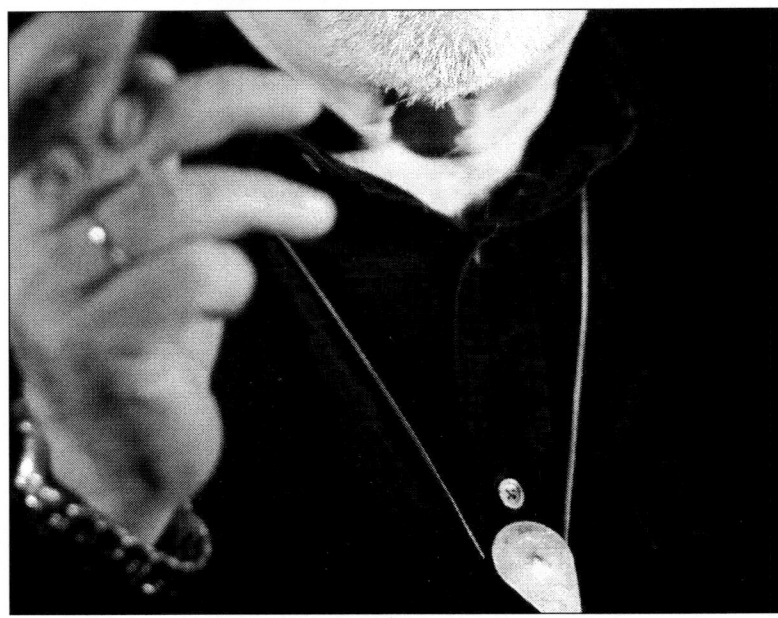

ABOUT
ART HISTORY

T wice named, twice exposed: 'Osvaldo,' transliterated from the Old German 'man from the South' into its Hispanic form. A translocated origin – the zero coordinate translated from North to South. 'Romberg,' the moniker originally borne by the inhabitants of any number of cities thus named. Yet cleft in

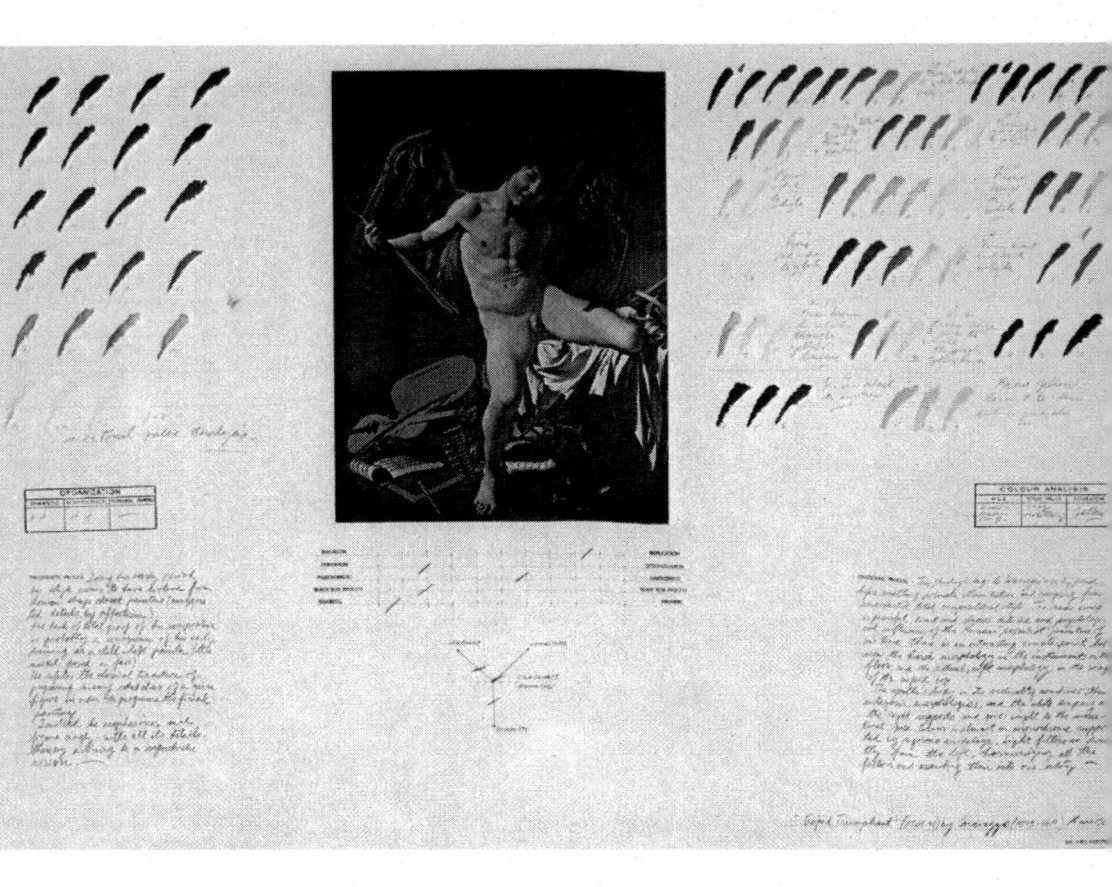

osvaldo romberg and the teaching of colors
MARCELIN PLEYNET

THE COURSE OF THE
AVANT-GARDE

Our idea of art has gone through a number of major upheavals in the course of the first three quarters of this century. A large part has no doubt been played by the evolution of society, artists' working conditions, and new methods of exhibiting and circulating art works, yet I would say that these are no more than epiphenomena. In my opinion the real cause of these major upheavals in our conception of art, as well as the myriad transformations of artistic form itself, lies in the progressive secularization of art. We can only consider our relationship with art today by taking into account its contemporary place, role, and function in our society. This can only be done insofar as we manage to grasp its relationship to the history that both

I come from Argentina and this explains everything. I never saw original paintings: we had fake Grecos and fake Courbets that I copied all the time. When I arrived in France for the first time, I took the train to Paris from Marseille, and went straight to the Louvre to see the paintings. By that time the Louvre was closed, so I went to Notre-Dame instead and to the Louvre the next day.

two, it could call forth the Hungarian for 'ruin' and the German for 'mountain.'
The former, a structure defined by the erosion of culture, the latter, a structure
defined by the erosion of nature, both utterly plotted, their locations unchang-
ing, keystones of situated knowledge. Osvaldo Romberg: twice named, twice ex-

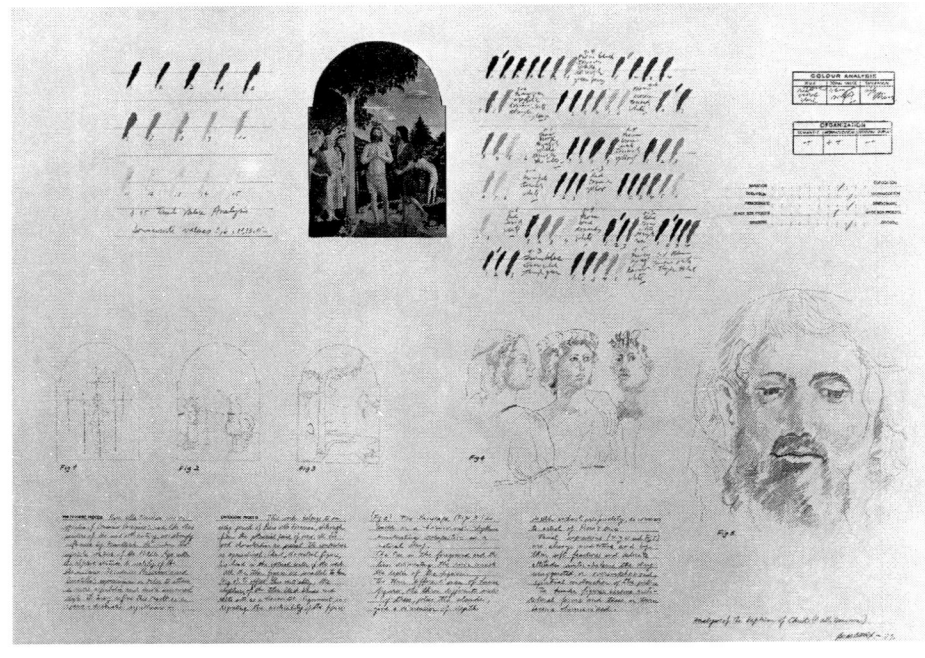

our art and our society have to some degree inevitably inherited. Quite obviously I am not going to begin the analysis of this history and its inheritance here. I will merely confine myself to the observation that from the outset right up until the present day, or more precisely up until the end of the nineteenth century, and this is true, in no matter which society and civilization we choose to consider, art has always been allied with religion. From the caves at Lascaux until the demise of the great art academies of the nineteenth century, which, it is well known, rested on the principles established by the Counter-Reformation and the Council of Trente, the place, role, and function of art was always more or less explicitly connected with the place, role, and social function of religion. The reappraisal and progressive disappearance of the explicit character of this partnership in a certain manner confronted art with itself and with the perpetual interrogation of its basis and justification for existence.

It is possible to conceive of the large number of avant-garde movements in this century as so many empirical attempts to provide a solution to this situation. The very notion of an avant-garde points to the headlong rivalry of these

When I was six, I went to my father's office - my father was a doctor at that time – and he had received advertisements, propaganda from various laboratories. There was a cat in one image. So I found a piece of wood, polished it, and then I painted the cat. Nobody believed I did it, not even my teachers, so they punished me.

I knew I would be a painter at that time. Still, I wanted to be a musician. I am better at music than at painting. But you do what you have to do, not what you want to do.

posed, riddled with natureculture. Renaissance painting was discovered not once but twice, in Flanders and in Florence. The advent of oils brought transportable culture to the party: for the first time, painters' masterworks could be applied to light canvases then set to travel the lands. Painting ceased to be site-specific; its

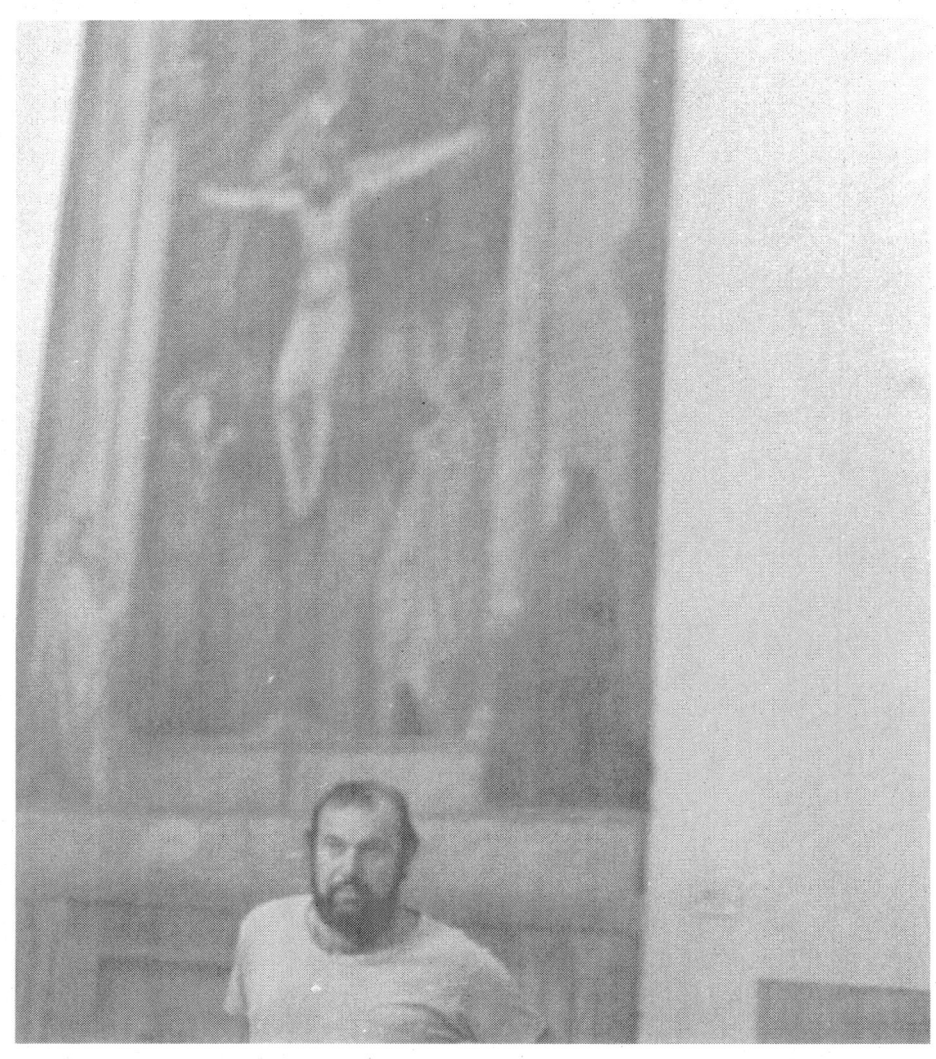

attempts. In fact, if we decided that this religious crisis which has marked the world of art was never actually recognized as such and in consequence was never more than implicitly experienced, and if we accept that art in any case can only reply indirectly to the questions it poses itself, we can easily understand that the resultant manifestations of this situation were at once an effort at self-interrogation and attempts to re-establish works of art on the basis of various hypothetical answers. In my opinion, the proliferation of artistic movements and avant-garde "schools" during the first three quarters of the twentieth century is nothing other than the manifestation of the empirical behaviour of art faced with the questions that it raises and encounters. It remains that if these avant-garde movements all betray the same symptom they do not do so in the same manner, and that today, when their very accumulation would seem to have exhausted the range of answers to the questions which motivate them for that very reason, it becomes possible to envisage a paradigmatic reading of them. Many artists today are troubled by this history of accumulated and in most cases heterogeneous fragments and are trying to find the means to understand and synthesize them. In this ef-

fort, their problem is obviously to find a key to what is contained in the diversity of this proliferation, and to locate and analyse the point in its chain where a set of terms can coalesce. Clearly neither the chronology nor the simple summation of the different movements, which together make up the history of the avant-garde in the first three quarters of the twentieth century, is at stake. For that we must situate ourselves at a point shared by all the groups alike. Such a point, it seems to me, is identified by the work of Osvaldo Romberg better than by any other.

Osvaldo Romberg's present works address themselves to stabilizing the eclectic pattern of avant-garde production through what I would see as a critical and analytical deployment of different, more or less successful, attempts to establish a new normative and academic code for modern art. It is impossible to speak of Osvaldo Romberg's present works without taking into consideration the whole background which they articulate. It can be seen from the brief summary above that this background, connected as it is to the theory of modern and contemporary art education, involves the sum total of what is generally called the history of modern

language ceased to be an articulation of its immediate surrounds; it developed a new language: the language of color. Caravaggio and Van Eyck spoke that language, their palettes became its evasive lexicon. O.R., the artist-traveller, teased those laurels from their historic guardians, giving color its voice and ac-

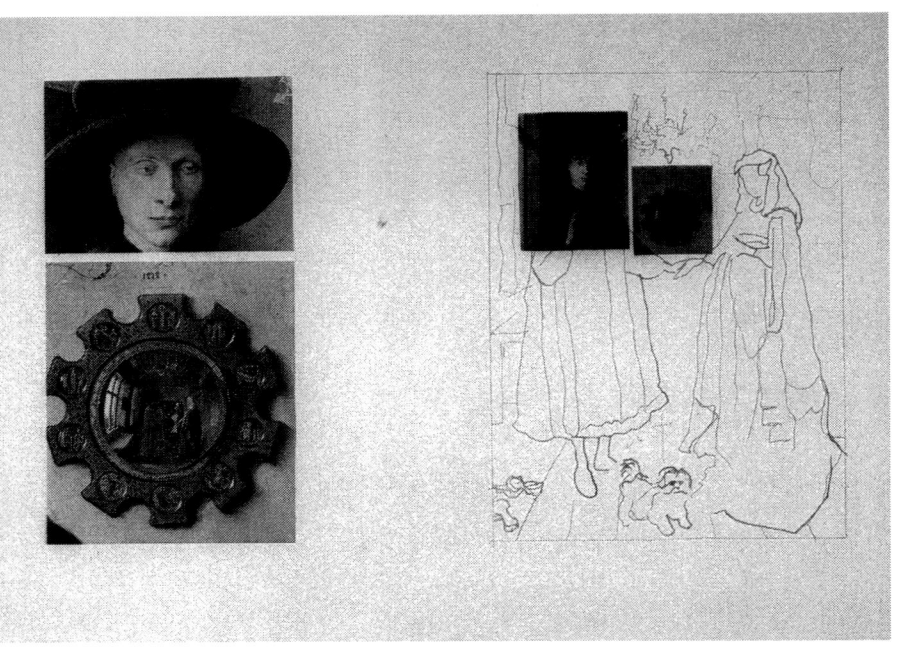

art. This said, the artist, who is fixated on the theory of education in general, could hardly adopt other means than a more or less efficient didactic discourse. By fixing attention within the limits of a general theory of education, that most specific "will to rationalization" that is enclosed in the theory of color, Osvaldo Romberg is able to propose a quasi-paradigmatic critical reading of the general discourse on art and its avant-gardes. He reveals his position, which is as original as it is simple, with perfect clarity in answer to a question by Ygal Zalmona: "Are you trying to formulate a system of laws from which we can derive other laws?" He replied: "Under no circumstances. I established no laws. I make use of some laws in the context of my work on mythology. For instance I use the chromatic circle but specifically as a neutral framework within which I manipulate the mythologies of color." On the basis of a perfectly irrational claim: "I pursue the pleasure of making things," his attitude to the theory of instruction and the theory of color permits the artist to uncover their mythological bases. To my knowledge, Osvaldo Romberg is the only artist to analyze and rework the symptoms which make up the avant-garde movements of modern art. Of course the terms "symptoms" and "my-

I am a commentator, and this is also very Jewish. My books are palimpsests. I believe in transparency (but this is Borges' influence of course).

I am sad that I cannot paint like Pavarotti sings. You can simply enjoy him. But I admire Diego Rivera because he has the capacity to express himself and make people feel as well. The art we do isn't only for us, otherwise it's just therapy.

cultured spectators fresh eyes to read. For years he dogged them, repeating the gestures of his antecedents with oil and canvas. He was a spirited artist and she was an unfaithful muse, reluctant to relinquish her four hundred year old flame. She was claimed by two masters whose differing ambitions were written

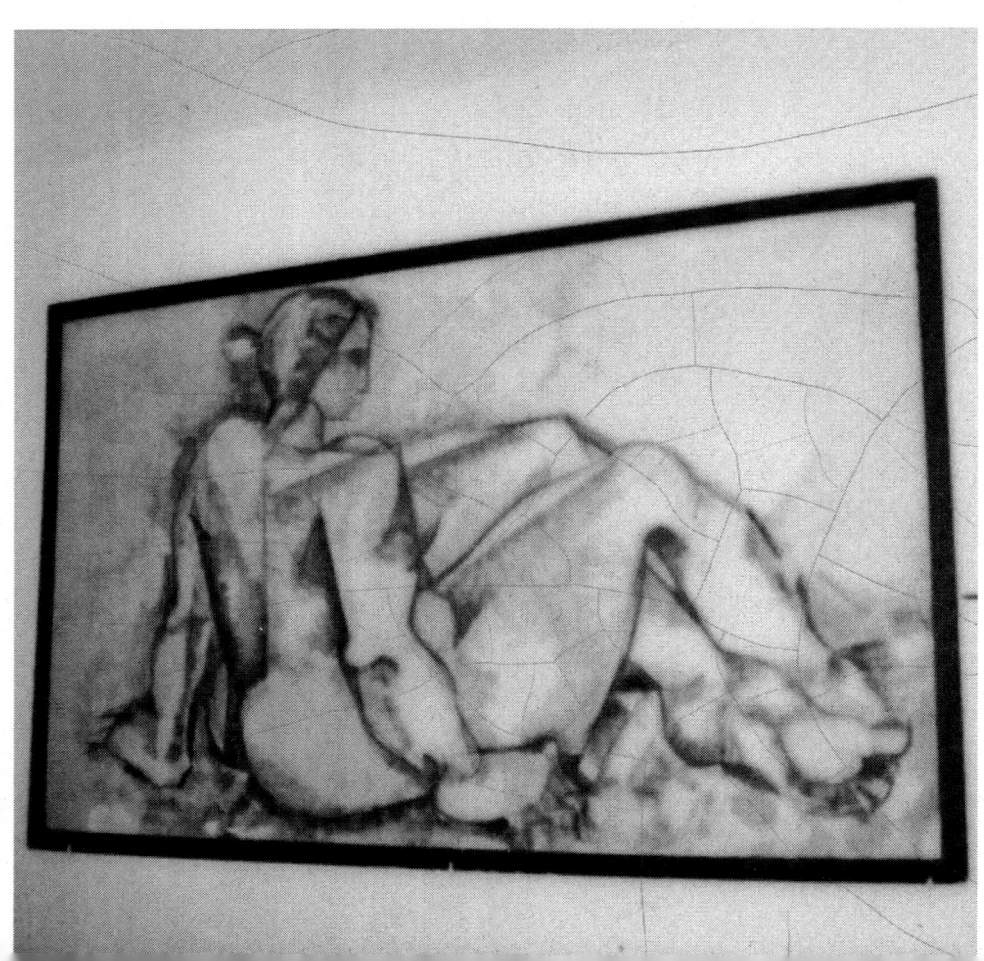

thology" do not suggest that the phenomenon under consideration lacks all other reality or relationship to the real; it is simply that by this very fact such a relationship to the real is diverted to short-term profits the fixation of which constitutes the symptom or the mythology. Consider the series Color Propositions Inside the Limits of their Tonal Value of 1978 (acrylic and pencil on paper); a group of varying sized marks, the trace production of which is very obvious, establishes and deploys the range of tonal value limitations of a certain number of colors. We could take this page at its face value as an exercise if it were not for the quality of each mark's production and the specific presence of the writing underlying this production of the name: vermillion, violet brown, etc. From the color to its name, from the mark's production to the specific graphic quality that takes on the same role as the production of the mark, the order of the real functions in a symptomatic deflection such that it becomes mythology: the work of art.

QUESTIONS ON COLOR

No matter how much he denies a pre-occupation with semantics, in the collection of tones that make up Osvaldo

Romberg's pieces it is impossible to be indifferent to the constant presence of the practice of writing. This writing, of course, makes play of its graphic, plastic qualities, but its purpose is also supported by the sense that it lends to each element (the name of the color which it accompanies) as well as the overall work. If we want to understand what is involved in Osvaldo Romberg's project, we must notice how the graphic quality of the word authenticates and lends its signature to the quality of the color. And here in my opinion is where we must look for the distinguishing mark between what, for example, Meyer Shapiro has called "the rationalism" of Seurat and the analytic "rationalism" of Romberg. Believing that color is subject to fixed laws, Seurat was convinced that these laws "can be taught like music." For his part Osvaldo Romberg, probably remembering Seurat's statement, has said, in a tone which can hardly fail to persuade us that he is not lacking in humor: "I am a frustrated musician." In fact the graphism, comprising color marks which it defines etymologically (cadmium yellow) and in otherwise indefinable sub-classifications (cadmium yellow plus white – cadmium yellow plus two whites, etc.), that accompany all of Osvaldo Romberg's pieces, suf-

in a palette unchanged. Steady and sure, and slightly macabre, the maverick O.R. would erase her face only to enlarge it and paint it anew. After a time, who could say what came first: erasure or imposture. Two years later, they were together again. She appeared unchanged, or was there a hint of something in

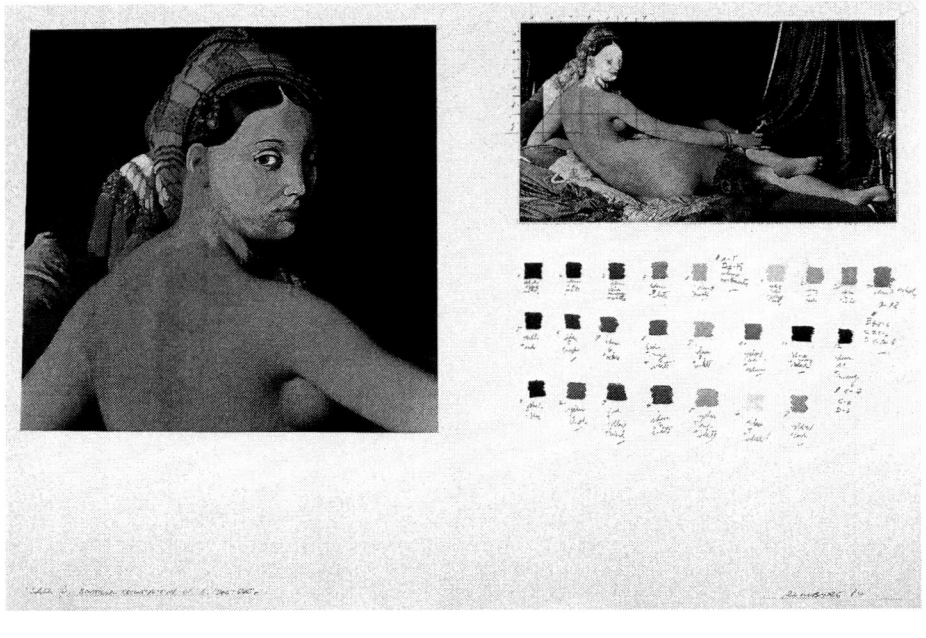

ficiently asserts that color cannot be taught like music and that it is "notated" quite differently. Certainly from each side of the reproduction of "La diseuse de bonne aventure" by Caravaggio, the "Margaritta Giovenetta" by Velasquez, the "Ménines" by Velasquez, the "Conversion de Saint Paul" by Caravaggio and many others of Osvaldo Romberg's analytic boards, color seems to establish itself in terms of chromatic tendencies. In any case these boards which refer quite clearly to exercises in color classification are accompanied by graphic definitions without which they would communicate nothing more than shimmering superficial effects. The construction of these analytic boards with their horizontal and elongated format and the whole which they make up should also be noticed: they comprise the reproduction of a painting which has marked the history of art with, on both sides, the nominal color range of its composition arranged in the linear order of a scriptural tendency towards discourse which signs and seals its definition. Just like the Color Classification Exercises, it is language and discourse which assume control of the determination and the inherent tendency of the painting and lend these pieces their specific significance. I want to insist on how the Color Clas-

I think that I can say some things only with painting.

Sometimes I paint auratically, and sometimes I paint without aura, making use of reproductions and transfers. It depends on the desired effect and strategy vis-à-vis the context of the contemporary art scene.

her eyes? He daubed a matrix of pink and purples atop her loins and with those fireworks she mouthed "L.H.O.O.Q." When next they met, she would speak no more, her mouth censored by a barrage of swatches. Is it really the same girl that O.R. thus veils? Is she a twin, or closely related? I do recognize that gaze,

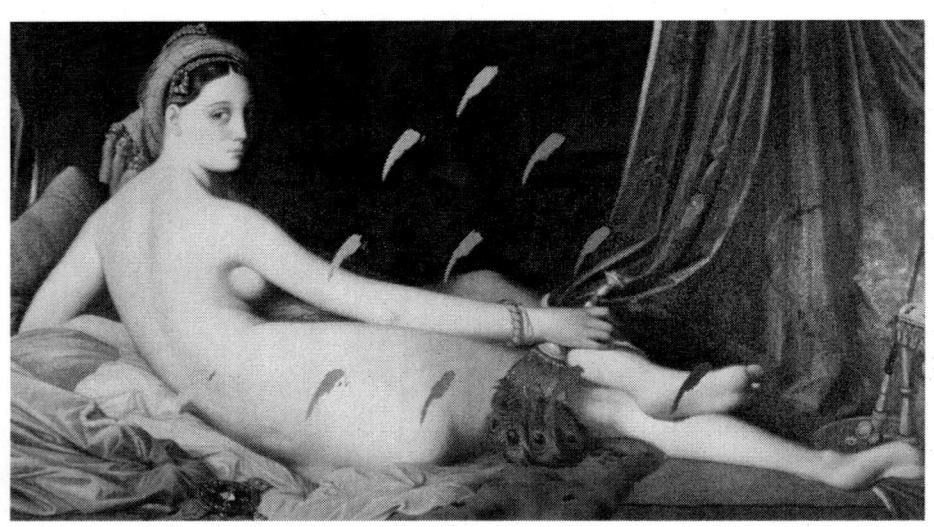

sification Exercises, and what I have called "analytic boards", intersplice each other, even if it is the former which finally impose their sense on the overall work. Osvaldo Romberg demonstrates without the least ambiguity that the laws of color are no longer subjected to an experimental scientific system but rather to a system of language. It is easy to imagine to what extent this transforms not only our outlook on modern art but our outlook on art theory and art in general.

Osvaldo Romberg is entirely justified in treating them as fables of language and reason – in other words as mythologies. In the "analytic boards" of works belonging to the history of art, the mythological function of color as seen in the questions arising out of the modernist avant-garde movements contaminates and compromises every approach to the history of art which is based on a twin repression – symbolic up until Leonardo da Vinci and afterwards scientific. These "analytic boards", which are composed by reference to a well-known work of art in reproduction are represented in three formal and graphic stages. The first two comprising color analysis and organization have the role of exposing what I would call, to use a notion from

My work probably has an intellectual quality. It requires you to have read a fair amount, to know about Malevich, etc. It's not easy to read without knowledge of contemporary and classical culture. In that sense, you could say that I am a modern artist.

and there's method in her sadness. She speaks in tongues: provenance is gone, taxonomy remains. She reminds me of another past flirt, whose language and posturing would bubble with enthusiasm: "I have always been a great lover of the Caravaggio. My heart begins racing and my step quickens whenever he

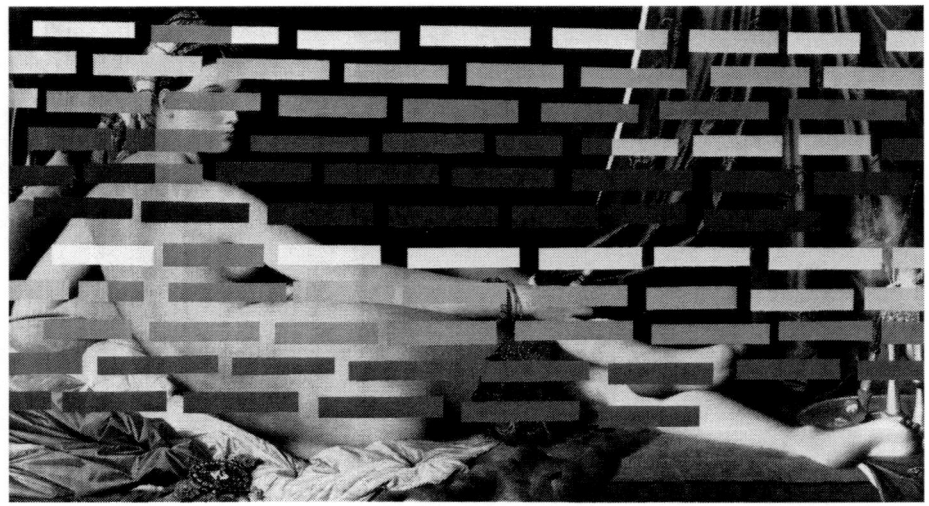

Roland Barthes, the color "mytheme" of the pictorial project of the picture in question. These two stages operate in the double philogenetic and ontogenetic categories of the discursive process that gives them meaning. The color "mytheme" in Osvaldo Romberg's work explicitly brings into play the genius of painting as history at the ontogenetic level and as language at the philogenetic level, and this through specification of color in relation to language. The two moments of this third stage formally occupy the whole lower half of the board with a dense graphism in such a way that the reproduction of the work under investigation seems to be definitively tilted towards the sense inherent in language and more specifically the language of Osvaldo Romberg, which here risks the analysis of his fixations through their encounter with the work which happens to have been chosen.

What is and what could be entailed in the resurgence of the return of the repressed in art? What is and what could be entailed in the discovery of free association that, through the intermediary of color, has linked man in all ages to the indefinably reconvertible order of the states and phenomena which he encounters? What name should we give to something that proposes to "think thought"? Osvaldo Romberg has managed to convince us today that this resurgence can also produce a work of art and that, while waiting to find out the exact significance of a name in a specific context, every work of art can carry its own.

comes near. I remember on one occasion, it must have been in winter, I was at the Quai du Louvre and I brushed past the master and flushed red with delight as I felt his eyes on my back. Turning around, I realized my foolishness, it was only his David looking on: a mere trick of the light. I often think of him, and

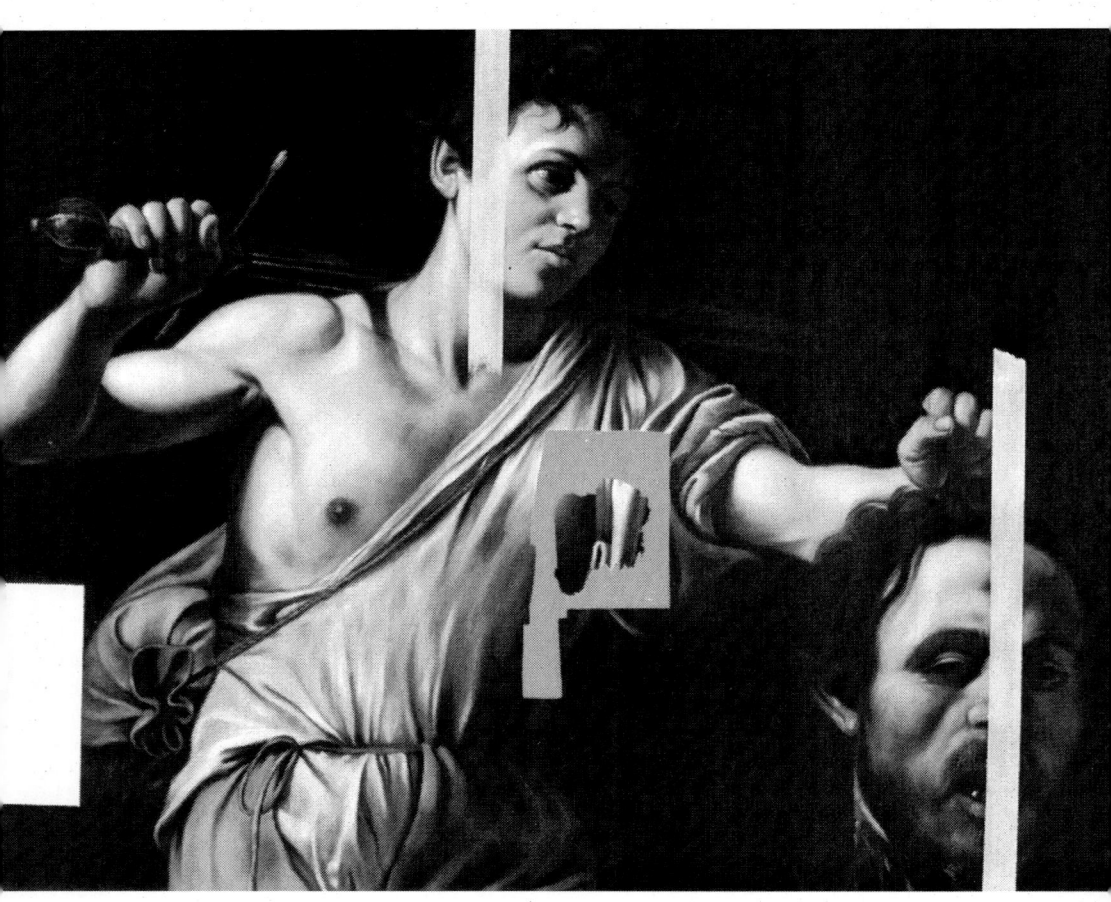

how to undo/redo the object by osvaldo romberg
MARJORIE WELISH

Artifact One: Draw a Circle. Think about it. *Artifact Two:* Draw a Circle. Name it zero. Think about it. *Artifact Three:* Point to Zero. Draw it. Think about it.

CONCEPTUAL ART

Artifact Four: Point to Zero. Draw it. Think about it. Write about it. Build that.

Remarkable about much Conceptual Art is that it is not abstract. It is often driven by a set of procedures concretizing forms of symbolic notation that would in themselves be abstract and as such entirely adequate to thought.

For those whose frames of reference allow it, zero is a mathematical, philosophical, theological and broadly cultural concept freighted with historical

The only way to make art is to try to resolve a problem, a sentiment, an emotion. The only way to teach is to see where the proto-artist is weak. The neurosis is there to resist culture, and the proto-artist can create his own being-in-the-world.

still believe his was the greatest charm, the greatest love. De La Tour was all talk, all dross: I never got anywhere beyond that falsely pious air he always sets about himself. It begs the question, whether his talent, and our love, was out of faith, zeal or application. I had such a rollicking time with Van Dyck, though:

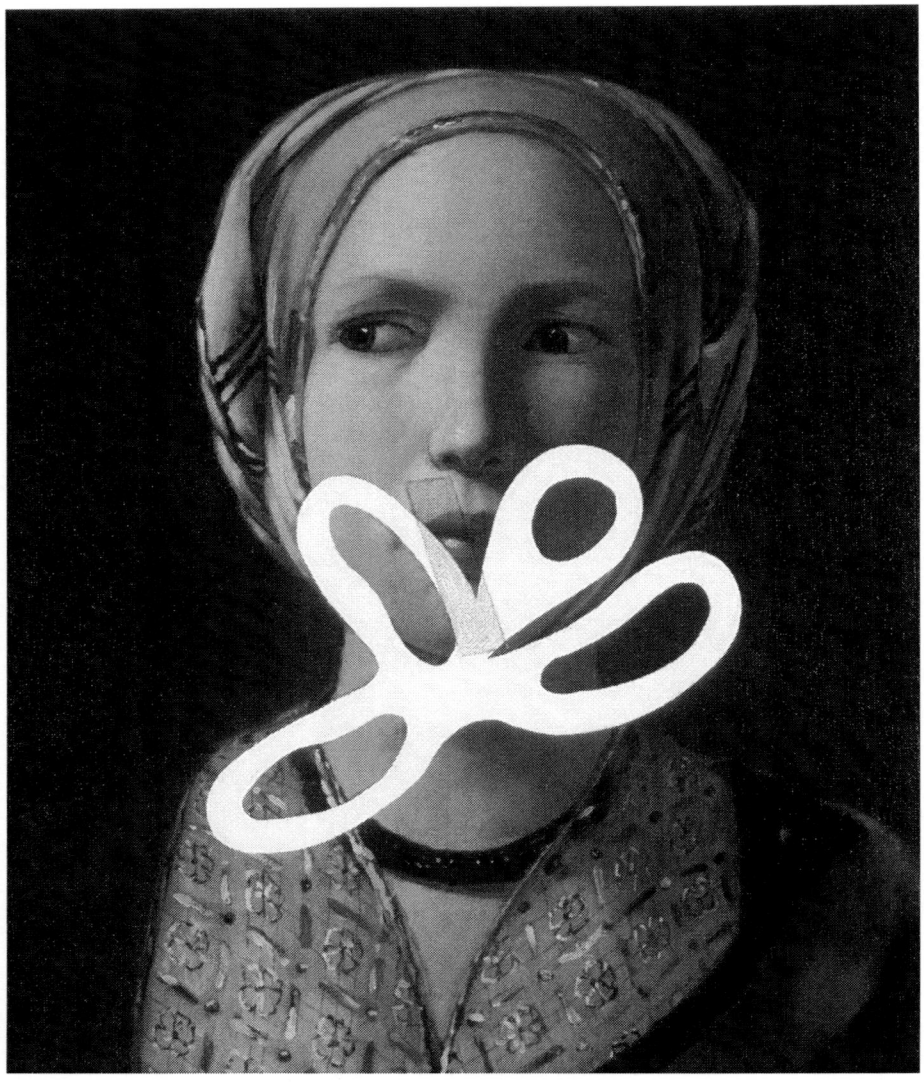

embodiment insofar as the archives on this matter inform us. It even has socio-economic heft, furthermore, as when in census, certain categories of the population are said not to exist. The point of all this is to establish that the notion named zero after its Italian adoption of the Arabic strong misreading of the Indian concept of blank has conveyed profound significance and complexity without having to be literally built.

The same might well be true for the shard of an artifact, as we have all seen in museums. Heavy with implicit text, this artifact, mostly corroded now and so with no form to speak of in æsthetic terms, is as eloquent at conveying cultural content as any – should the viewer acknowledge the content. Materially scant, weighing perhaps only as much as a few grains, the artifact in question may read as replete with the following methodologically-framed information: technology: metallurgy; structural design: fibula; style: Scythian; culture: Central Asian, nomadic. The shard is as marked as it ever needs to be for those who read visual culture to apprehend, discern and comprehend some significant complex of meaning even as it remains perennially open to interpretation.

And, again, the same is true for abstract painting of the decisive formal and cultural complexity of, say, Malevich's "Black Square." Unbuilt or materially scant, all these cultural objects speak eloquently of their contexts criss-crossed with heterogeneity and historicity; and, so introduced, they may be said to be accessible to interpretation that reflects the perennially hypothetical nature of empirical inquiry.

These artifacts, then, are not static, are not reified, are not subsisting on decorative triviality, except insofar as our minds do not know how to animate them.

OSVALDO ROMBERG'S ARTIFACTS IN RELATION TO CONCEPTUAL ART

Relative to this paradigm of the cultural object, Romberg has made palpable objects, yet rather than leave interpretation to be thought, he has made the interpretive aspect as well, and so through this construction has rendered explicit that implicit interpretive content.

Indeed, Conceptual Art in Romberg's hands has incorporated what might be called the lecture-demonstration into

56 | *he was a wonderfully astute soul: he knew the value of things, and people, and his presence, as much as his work, really brought that out on canvas, and then into his pocketbook. What adventures we had! Portrait, artist, sitter and specta-tor so reliably indulged." Many years later, she wrote to me on a much sadder*

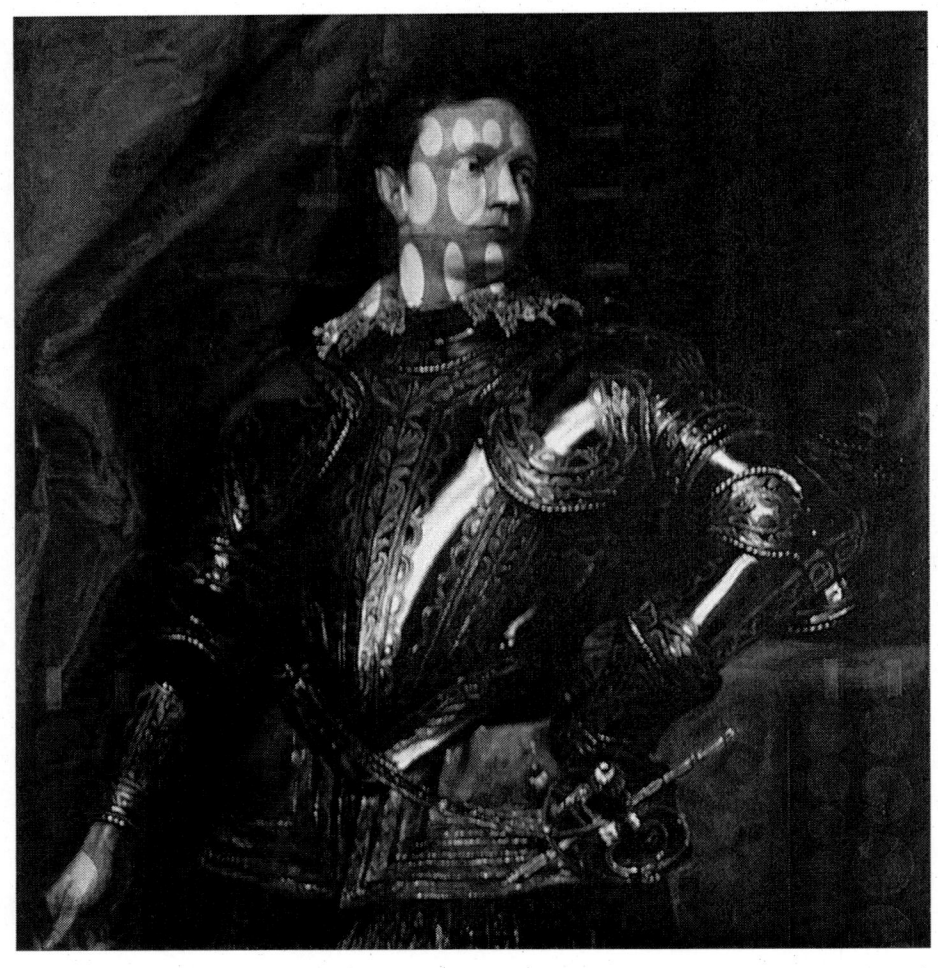

the artifact itself. Putting it another way, his are artifacts comprised of second-order discourse physically and pictorially constructed and marked with terms of address. It is sometimes claimed that for the Productivist cell of Rodchenko-Stepanova that it created a new format for the book, and that the photo album became the instrumentality for reading the collective rhetoric in the hands of the unlettered. Whether in or out of its slip-case, the photo album as object concretized forms of symbolic notation adequate to thought – albeit somewhat coercively. Still, as much as their talking books dramatized the word and spoke to the public in advocacy of reading, the photo album entered the world and spoke to the public on behalf of ideas. Romberg's objects engage this didactic function with course corrections made for differing politics.

Even so, in the face of those for whom looking at formal art is either pretentious, meaningless, or both, it might be argued that Romberg's objects teach the lettered how to read a visual thing. For those who read, and are more comfortable contemplating literary rather than visual statements, Conceptual Art offers guidance in how to parse the image and attend to the implications of its grammatical undoing. Taxonomic schema

No, my art isn't political. I participated in politics, in history with my body. I participated in revolutions with students in Argentina against Perón, and in the evolution of Israel.

58 | *tone, though her sensibility remained. "Dear Theo; Ever since the wall came down I feel a certain wariness in me. So much has been spilled over the years: tears, blood, bad ink on bad paper. No more great daubs of red on every public building, but still I worry: my tired eyes fear the black and white images from*

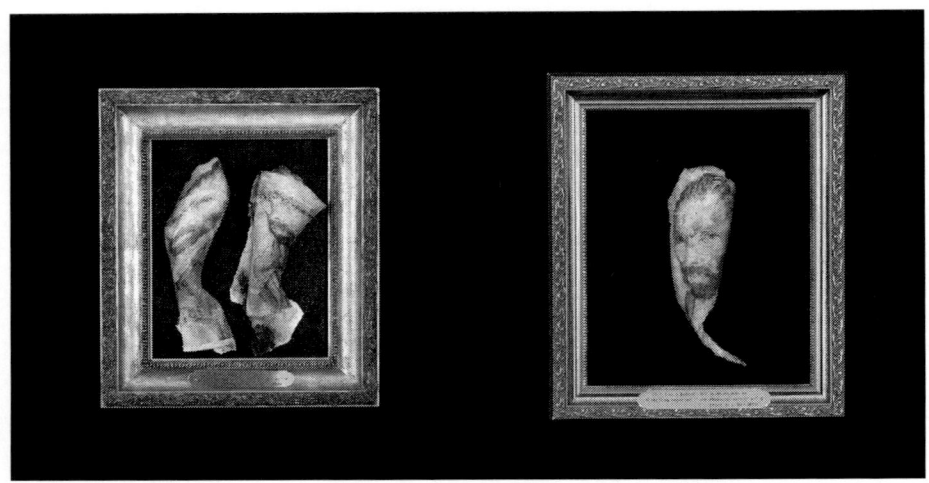

mediate the verbal and visual realms of utopic knowledge, and Romberg answers Malevich's charting of form and style, Joseph Albers's charting of color, and Ad Reinhardt's giving slide lectures on world art histories, by committing to spreadsheets (or to the projected fantasies spreadsheets would have) his anti-foundational analysis of art history. Though built, his artifacts are meant to be read, are made for those who engage knowledge in written form first.

Informed through literary sources in critical theory, artifacts produced under this ægis would show art history to be a fiction: well then, would Romberg entertain showing the fictions of critical theory? The anti-foundational foundational assumptions of contemporary post-modernity are well known to all of us, and Romberg, subscribing to these, generates irrepressible fictions that would undermine the cultural narratives we accept as valid, reasonable, even true. It may also be argued that the literary interpretative frameworks assume foundational positions in œuvre, however restlessly.

Familiar to other cosmopolites – especially those displaced or in diaspora, like Öyvind Fahlström and Kes Zapkus – is

I left to Israel in 1973, planning to stay for only one or two years. I'd been there before and was in love with early Israel as a social experiment. So I went back to Israel in March 1973 and began to teach. I thought I'd go back to Argentina after one or two years, but the situation there just got worse and worse and so, of course, I didn't go back. I visited Argentina to see my sister and father, when he was still alive, and I still go back every year to visit.

60 | *America. They smear at their edges. I keep catching my eye in the mirror these days. At different times, and in different places, I see the same other in that reflection. I wiped my mouth on a napkin this morning just to see what stain my face would leave. This gesture, the consequent smearing, second nature to the*

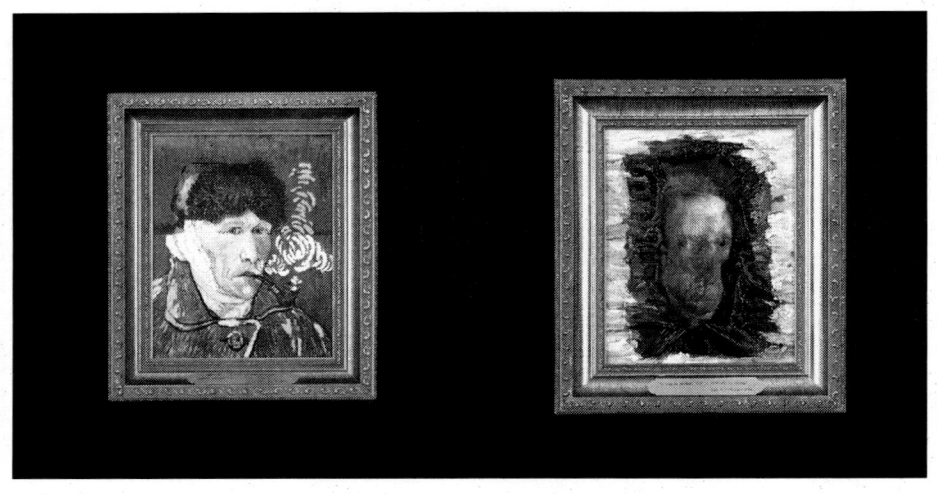

the art of disequilibrium and so it is no wonder to find with Romberg a cosmopolitan world view that is "crazy for culture," remaining in perpetual quest and even tantalized by an ideology of adventure. As Michael Nerlich says, "adventure in a chance-determined world" is at last a proposal for contingency, the contingency of history and circumstance wreaking havoc with universal knowledge. It is a disruptive factor and, if an exploitative impulse, Romberg's adventure has also been the instrumentality for expressive strategies of the counterculture.

LATIN AMERICAN
CONCEPTUAL ART

Recognition of the international perspective on Conceptual Art is slow in coming to the United States even as individuals from abroad enjoy considerable respect. So it was news to us when in 2000 the Queens Museum of Art threw its weight behind the exhibition "Global Conceptualism: Points of Origin, 1950s – 1980s", and with its three project directors and eleven specialists mounting an assault on our ignorance, cooperatively explained the several leading ideological æsthetics from around the world selectively chosen to represent the international scope of Conceptual Art.

You cannot actually speak of the end of anything. As the Romans sat in their baths, and the barbarians were coming from the East, I'm sure one Roman said to another, "this is the end of the world." We say the same things now of Islam and other phenomena. Apparently, the world did not end; civilizations go on and on. Other civilizations are no doubt currently discussing the imminent end of the Occident.

Who would have thought that the USSR would fall?

civilized man, didn't lessen my anxiety but heightened it, a salivating snapshot in its picture frame. At night, I have taken to dreaming of sunlight. During the day, I often think of the dark night sky. There seems to be no escaping its expanse, etched black and white onto the paper of this letter, verity smeared like so many

Although some of us had followed the cultural trajectories of Conceptual Art originating in language to address art or art world institutions and the contest between this group of artists and those keen on driving a Leftist wedge in the form of social critique, perhaps the most lasting effect of this show was that each of the essayists took curatorial charge of a rhetoric defining a body of objects, so that the centers of Australia and New Zealand became indistinct from that of Soviet Russia, which in turn manifested itself as distinct from Japan, which told of a position different again from that of Latin American Conceptual Art. The saleswoman in the shop reported that the catalogues of this massively attended show had nearly sold out.

The ramified response to coercive social discourse is certainly a distinction to be drawn when considering even the heterogeneity of artworks in Argentina. When Osvaldo Romberg said that he was happy to appear before the audience of students rather than that of the art world, it was not a courtesy. And when he recalled sparring with a curator who had cast doubt on the ambition of the work, and Romberg insisted that this work is a true expression of Argentinean cosmopolitanism, that was

I am a Jew and, though I am not religious, I am happy to be a Jew. I spent a big part of my life in Israel, and I still go there ever year. Many of my former students are now prominent there.

shadows on the window panes outside. It is hard to hear in the mornings, the voice of last night's histories calling me forward." I never heard from her again. With the passing of time, her face, story and handwriting would become blurred. Much like Stendhal's mirror, I saw the failure in my memories, but none in myself, as if senility bore no link to wrinkles and the circle none to its outline.

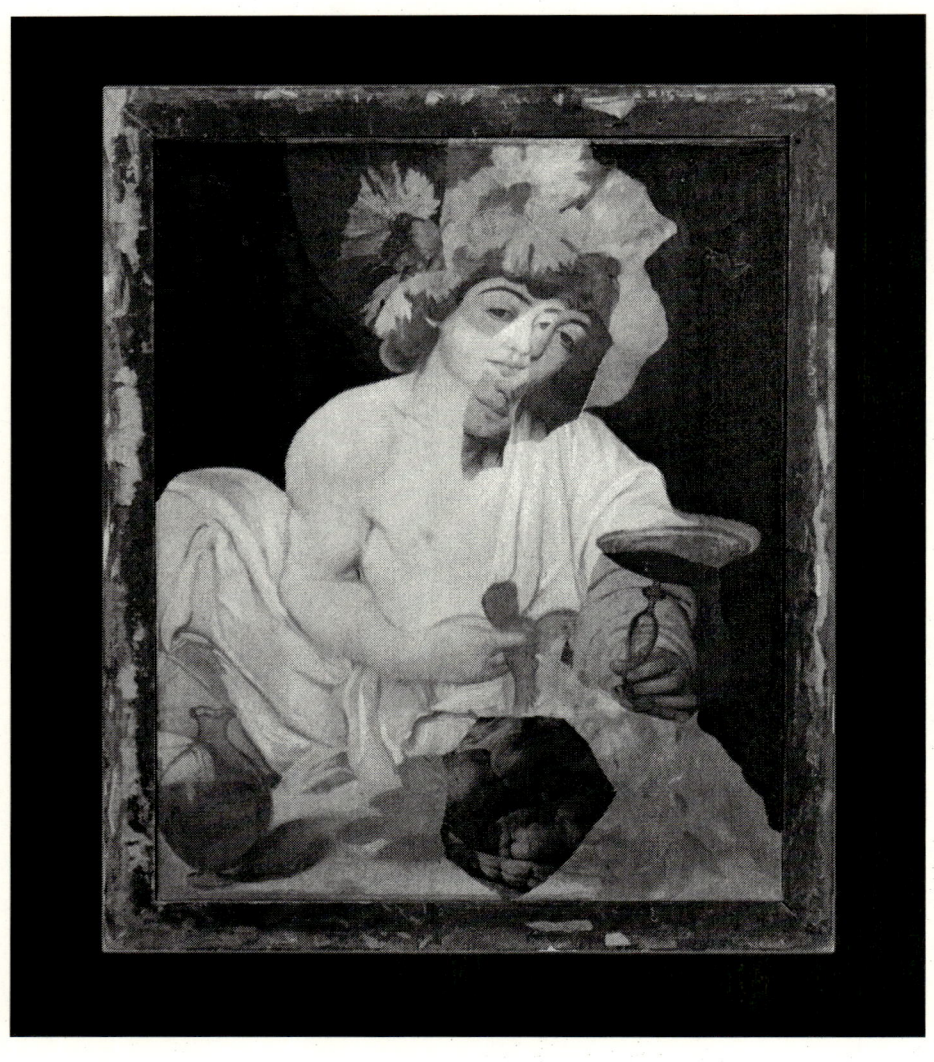

not a defensive reflex. Cosmopolitanism as a mode of inquiry is being advanced as a personal freedom and human right inscribed in his work as well as in his words. Let us learn from him. How to undo then redo the object to render cultural information open to view – and readied for productive insubordination – is at issue.

Why assume certain cultural artifacts in museums are intellectually simple if they have few if any moving parts? Why assume physically simple objects are those whose economy of means is parsimonious. Point to a simple artifact: indeed, in what sense simple, against which those artifacts technically and technologically elaborated are intellectually complex? Aren't you as discussants vulnerable to taking material appearances too literally (assuming that if materially scant, the artifact is culturally scant)?

I adore the social democracy of the kibbutz. I cannot be a communist because I can't stand the idea of dictatorship. The kibbutz was a good example of socialism. I don't care about money, about the power of ruling somebody's life. I only want the power to do what I want with my own life. In 1957 I was in the kibbutz Kfar Zsold. I would work hard in the kibbutz, in the fields and in the fish pools: I would wake up at 5am to go to the fields to work. Now, I wake up at 6am every day to go to my studio.

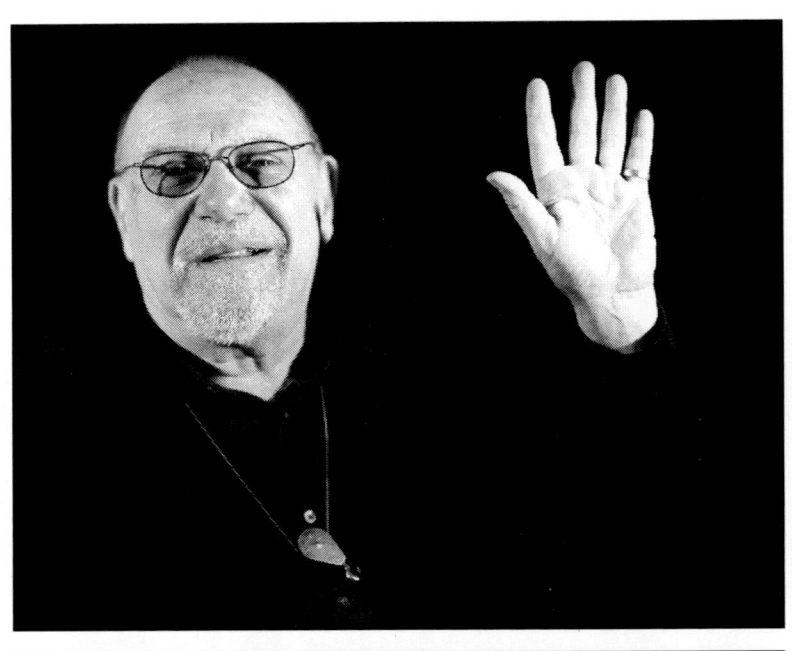

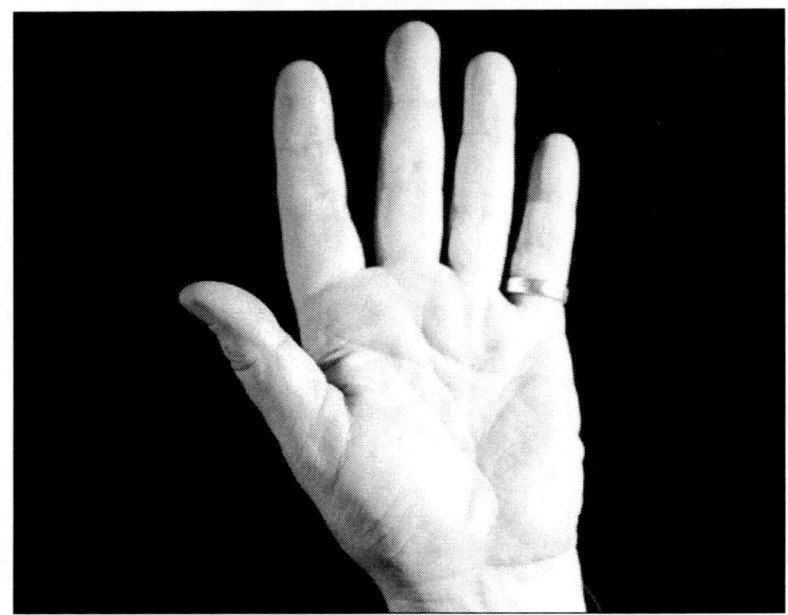

ABOUT
ARCHITECTURE

"This is it, this is where it starts." The Japans of my mind lay at my feet like so many soft facts of geography. Art, over here, all started with woodcuts and rituals, I'd been led to believe. For all those academic illustrations — always, the

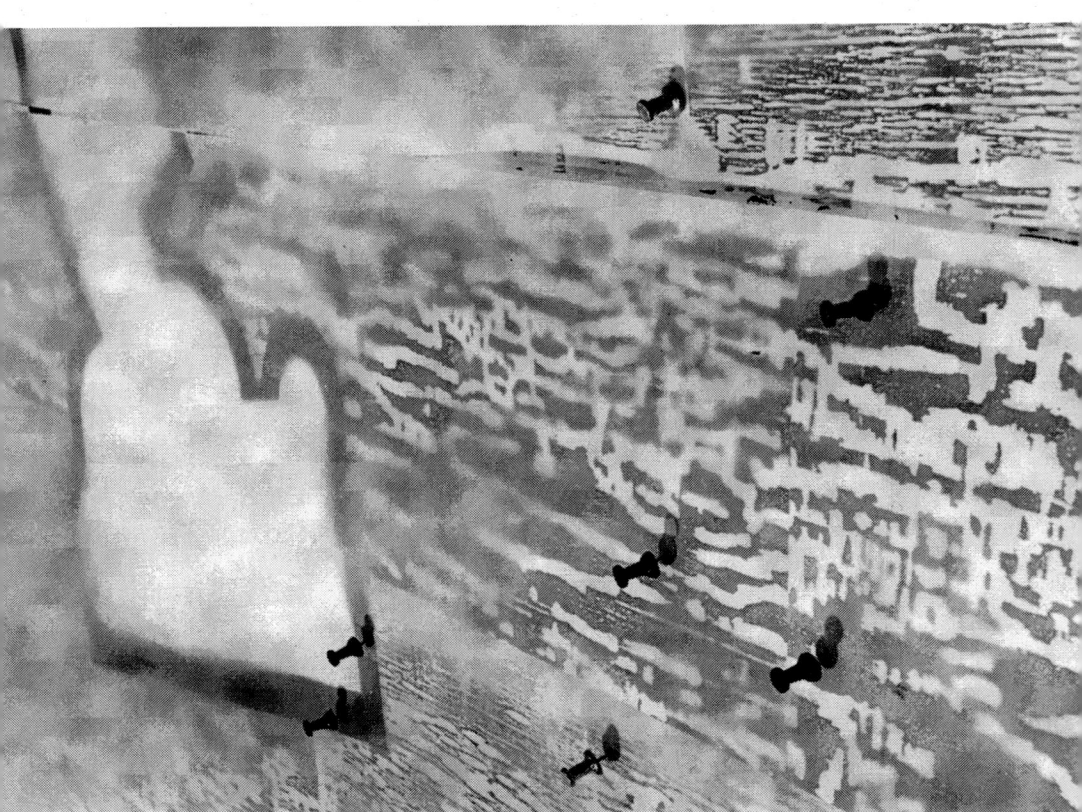

osvaldo romberg, the bauhaus and the spiritual
HENNIE WESTBROOK

Osvaldo Romberg's career spans more than thirty years as an artist and teacher. His vocation took him from his native Argentina to Jerusalem and from Jerusalem's Bezalel Academy to the Pennsylvania Academy of Fine Art.

During his tenure at the Bezalel Academy from 1973 as a teacher and from 1976 as its director, he put the curriculum on a more systematic and rational basis. An important legacy of the Bauhaus experiment was the systematic way of working that was applied in its workshops. In contrast with the Bauhaus, however, Bezalel's systematic methods bore fruit with its students: most Israeli artists of renown today studied at the Academy during Romberg's period of office.

In his early works in the seventies, Romberg experimented with color, liberat-

Borges influenced me a lot. My generation is a specific generation – we were also very influenced by the French. When I was 18, Sartre was king – Argentina was then dominated by French culture. Bachelard and Valéry were also influential, and Lévi-Strauss and Barthes. Proust too.

These are still my influences; It is very difficult to change the basic ideas you acquire when you first come into culture.

communion of water and rock, geology and civilization — the island still struck me as untamed. The gauntlet lay before me and I had the instruments through which to run it. The mere scratching of the sextants of yore would dissipate in the face of

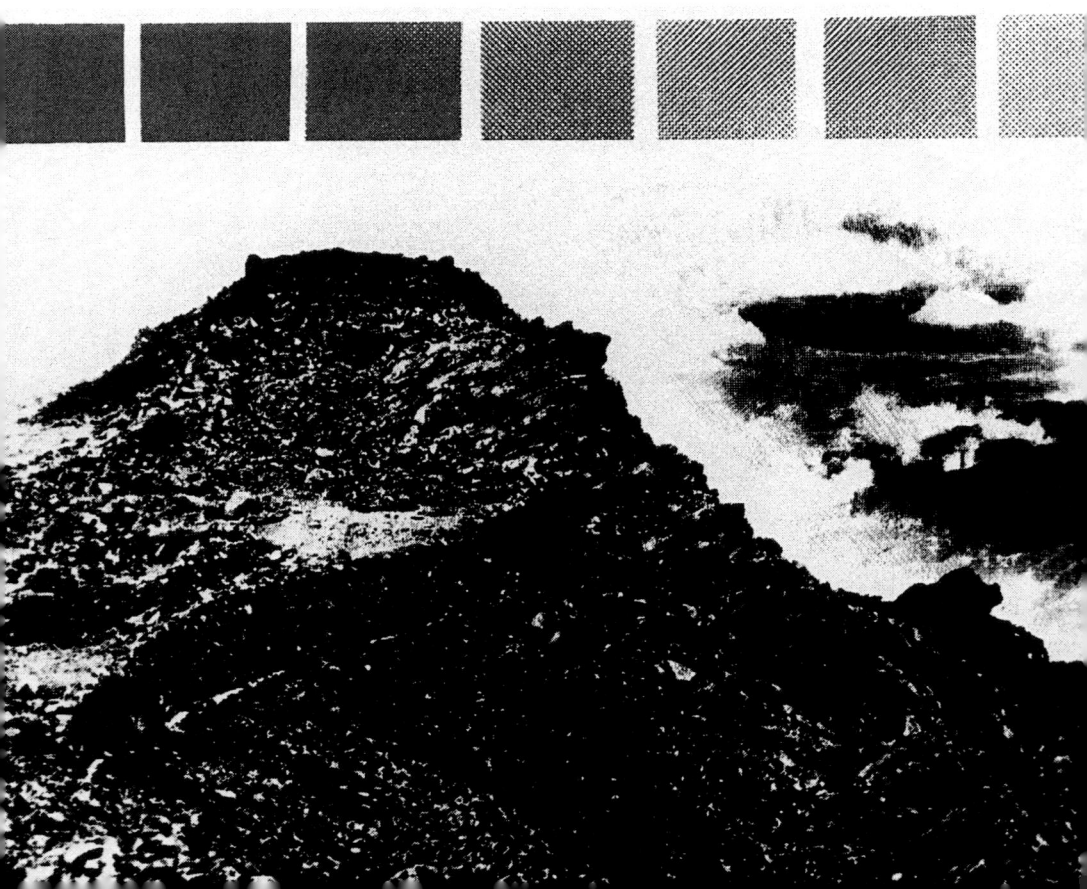

ing it from its dependence on form. In his installation *Color Environment* at the Bauhaus Archiv Berlin in 1982, he deciphered the floor plan of Brunelleschi's Pazzi chapel by superimposing it on the Gropius Bauhaus Archiv. As a reference point Romberg utilized Josef Albers' "Interaction of Colors". He created color charts on one of the walls which refer to the 'modernist grid', evoking a similar method to that used in his analysis of paintings in his *Mythologies* series.

The Bauhaus Archiv installation prefigures several ideas which he has elaborated in his subsequent works. On the one hand it contrasts and compares buildings, divided by time and brought together in the same space and to scale. On the other hand, it stages a confrontation between the sacred and the institutional.

In the late eighties, these ideas generated the exhibitions that he called *Building Footprints* and *On Scale*. Romberg's method was to detach architecture symbolically from its function and reduce it to a sign that can become an abstract sculpture, while still preserving its embedded cultural and historical significance. Romberg created objects which originated in diverse periods and cultures. These were attached to the wall or freestanding. Through his interventions, new associations and connections emerge which promote the discourse between art history and culture.

One of the tenets of the Bauhaus manifesto reads: "The ultimate aim of all creative activity is the building." In Romberg's creations, the historical building becomes merely the backdrop for new architectural sculptures. *Building Footprints III*, shown at the Vienna Museum of Contemporary Art, Stiftung Ludwig, in 1993, illustrates his method. In this exhibition, wooden reliefs based on the floorplans of historical buildings like the Roman Forum, the Temple of Amun at Luxor and the Erechtheion in Athens are fixed to the wall. These are complimented by floor plans of the remains of the same structures attached to drawing boards. Through subtle manipulations of surface decoration and hanging arrangement these objects projected an alternative meaning, expressing and interpreting the history of modernism. Furthermore, Romberg constructs a 1:1 floor plan of the Erechtheion out of bricks running through the museum. Seen against the baroque Hercules Room, the installation sets up the visual spectacle of a one-to-one confrontation between Classical Antiquity and the Baroque Age.

my excavations. The target sighted, I made the first cut, breaching boundaries like a slab of concrete turned keystone. Conquest followed conquest, as sure as history disrobed. It was not power I sought, nor exoticism I desired, nor even the need to

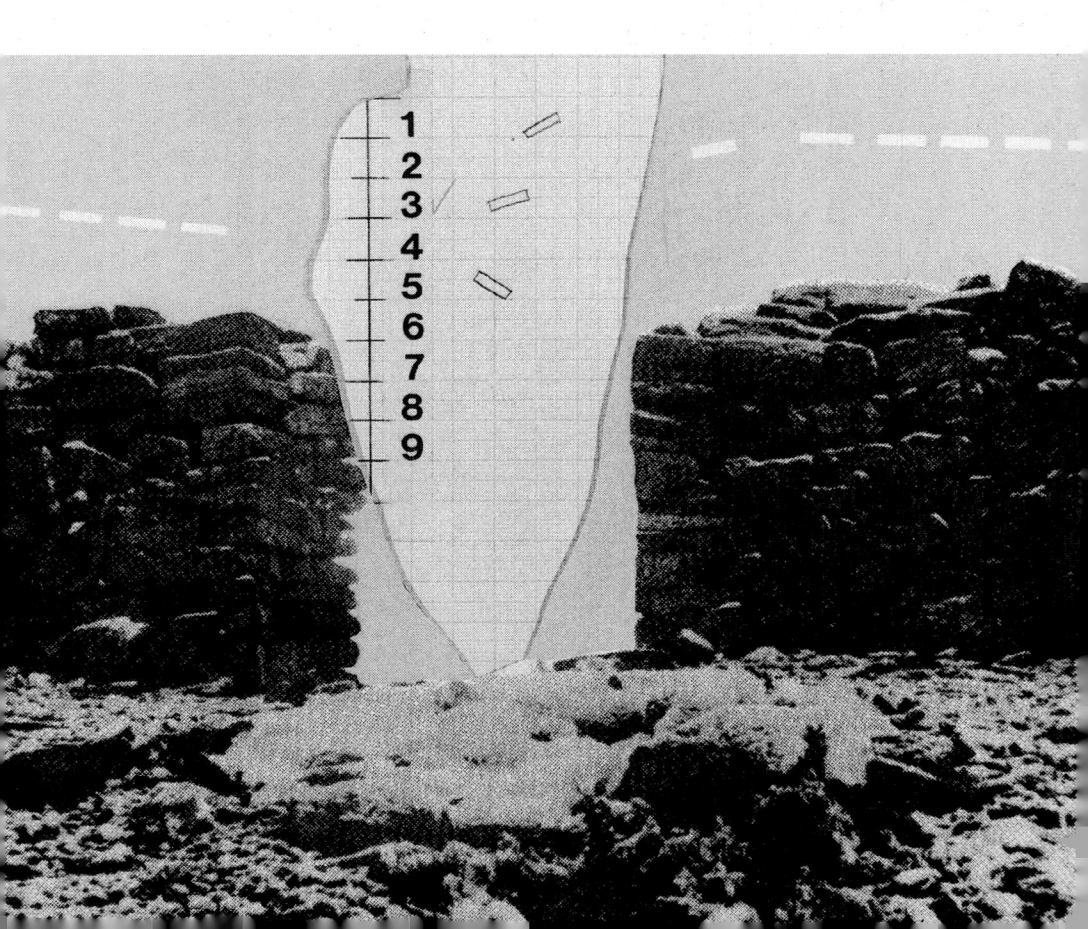

This part of the project is a reference to the *On Scale* exhibitions shown at both the Wilhelm Lehbmruck Museum in Duisburg and the Sprengel Museum in Hanover. In the latter, he examines church architecture of different ages and culture – from early Christian to the Corbusier Chapel in Ronchamp.

In the cold light of the Museum space he investigates culture through its choice of sacral spaces. Here Romberg intersects the Lehmbruck Museum space with the floor plans of Bernin's St. Andrea in Quirinale in Rome, extending it outside, suspended on thin columns, beyond the second story wall of the gallery. As in Vienna, the viewer experiences visually and almost physically the intersections of Western culture.

In the logical progression of the artist's works there are some which were seminal for new ideas and directions in his œuvre. One example is *Color Environment*, described above. Another is *The Last Mikvah on Fifth Avenue*. Installed in the Jewish Museum, New York, in 1990, the work prefigures the intersecting of spaces, analyzing a Jewish ritual space in order to comment on the cultural and the spiritual, and in this case, also the political. The ground plan of the ritual bath,

If you understand Derrida completely, then you will just do an illustration of Derrida. It becomes constipating. If you want to read something, read it fast. To read analytically is fine for scholars perhaps, but an artist should read fast, and understand creatively and incompletely. If you render text into parts, fragment it, then you enter the realm of floating meaning. Imagine how rich this is for an artist. What we do all the time, in every work of art, is to make indeterminate meaning as much as we can.

stake a claim. I was merely looking, de-scripting ground passed with eyes and writing too. I could see the women cavorting through the windows, unaware that they were naked. I accumulated samples as I went, they gradually metastasized into a

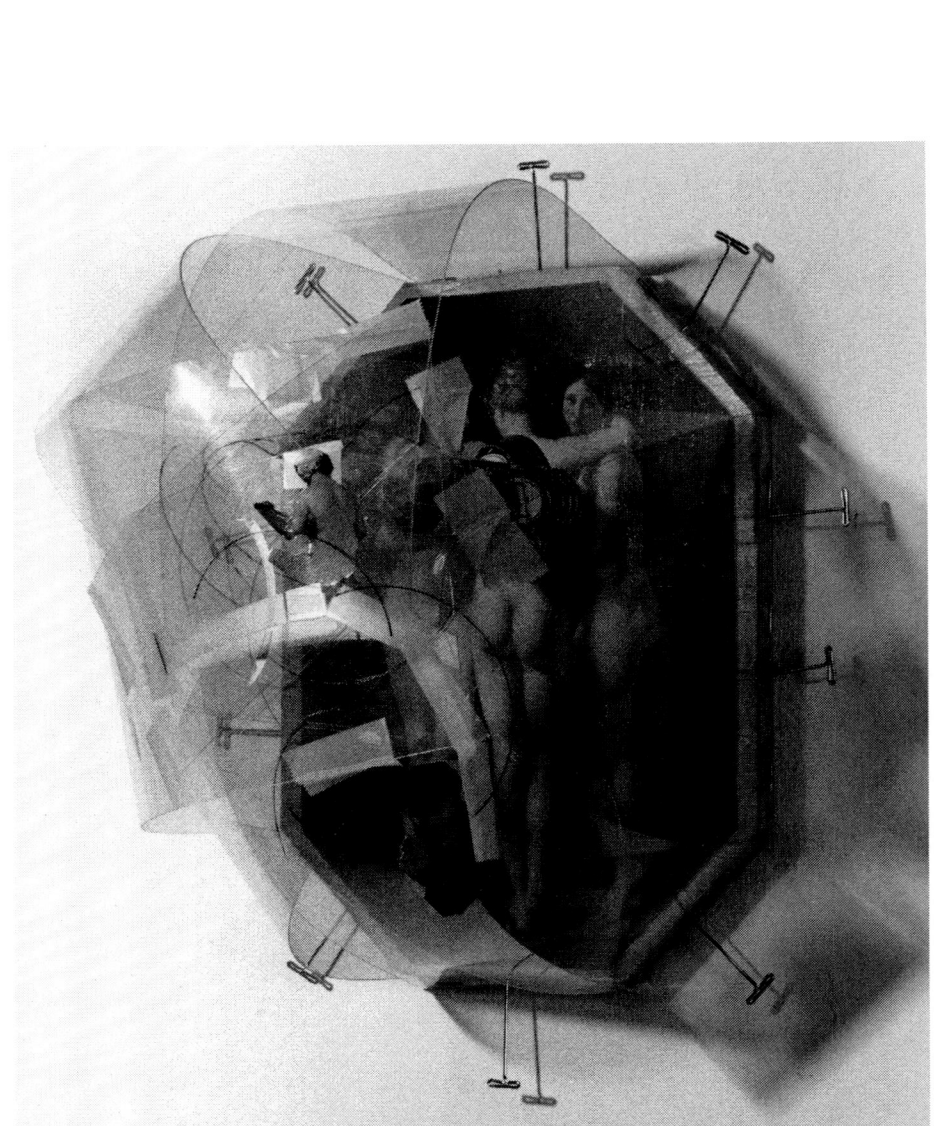

or mikvah, of Masada is constructed partly in the Museum courtyard and partly in the Museum proper. The actual remains of this ritual bath were excavated at Masada, the fortress that was the site of the last Jewish resistance against the Roman occupation in 73 BC. Romberg begins the investigation of the spiritual with a Jewish ritual space before turning his attention to mainstream cultures. The major part of the installation is the outside projection, leaving only a small part to represent the inner persona. It raises questions of cultural and spiritual survival and conflicts between opposing priorities. Thus the work communicates a very personal problem of the artist.

"The Last Mikvah" could be seen as a transition to the Macchu Picchu series. These installations consist of life-sized footprints of sections of the religious center of the Incas at Macchu Picchu in Peru. The footprints are transplanted into different environments (the Negev desert, Venice, St. Etienne in France). By altering certain elements within the building, like the axis – making it face Jerusalem or the Amazon jungle – he creates a dialogue or meta-narrative within the work itself. The Inca culture was annihilated, a fact to which Romberg alludes most strongly in his *Last Macchu Picchu*

I do not read like a scholar. I read like I am seeing fiction. You digest and you produce, and the same process happens in the mind of an artist.

Art is not theory. Art is objects, images, etc., that drag you to another place. A good piece of art doesn't absorb you, but throws you to another place. Theories absorb you and art propels you.

What I'm trying to say is that basically, I don't think so much.

collection. What at first were but quarries, soon became a quandary as I grasped the arches over them: they were each mere plots narrating a grid, the iron blue-print of London's Crystal Palace. Yet for sturdy construction, its Great Exhibition

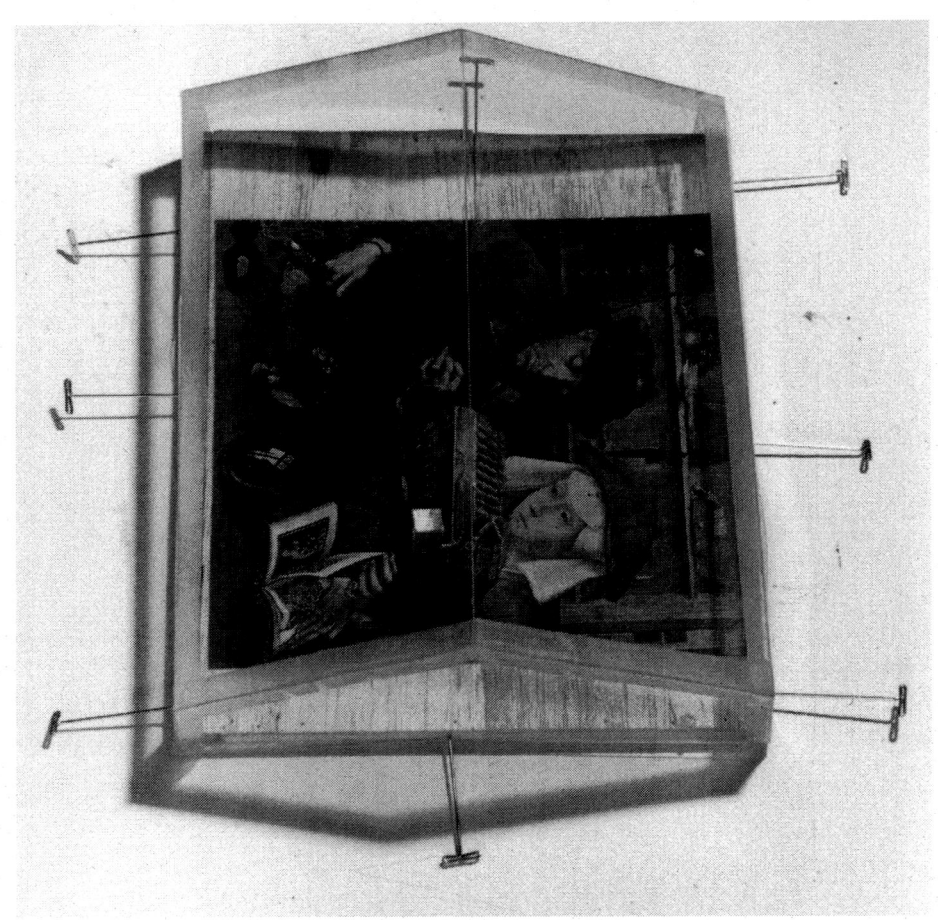

shown at St. Etienne. In the structure, erected outside the Museum, the viewer encounters excavation pits, covered with glass, through which the buried remains of fossils, shells and photographs are just visible. Also in the pits are stills of movies by Werner Herzog: "Aguirre Wrath of God", "Fitzcarraldo", and "Caspar Hauser." These films deal with subjects close to Romberg's heart and art: destruction of the mad conquerer, culture versus nature, and the savage versus the tamed. In addition, Romberg installed an oven which progressively consumed the paper building blocks of the installation. The ashes resulting from the burning were returned to their original location. This project enabled Romberg to fashion a work where the presentation and its critique are inextricably interwoven, a kind of "Gesamtkunstwerk" of text and critique, or as he would say: narrative and meta-narrative. The destruction of this culture is recorded on film interspersed with fragments of the Herzog movies, warning of future holocausts. The film was shown throughout the duration of the exhibition.

The Macchu Picchu series addresses problems of the last decades of the twentieth century and into the future: postcolonialism, globalisation and other cur-

I do teach my students, but the relationship is egalitarian. Through teaching I resolve problems of my own. I never teach anything I know, and this requires you to write a new text. When I work with assistants, my assistants see my grammar. They can use it, or they can be against it; They can reinforce me, or they can weaken my work. And when they weaken my work, I have to understand the challenges in my work.

A work is always collective, even when you are alone.

was temporary. Cardinals, regents, diplomats and queens arrived in hordes: now termites, now bees. The great white was lost in the middle of momentary organic complexity, but it is in the nature of walls to fall. For symmetry is as fleeting as a

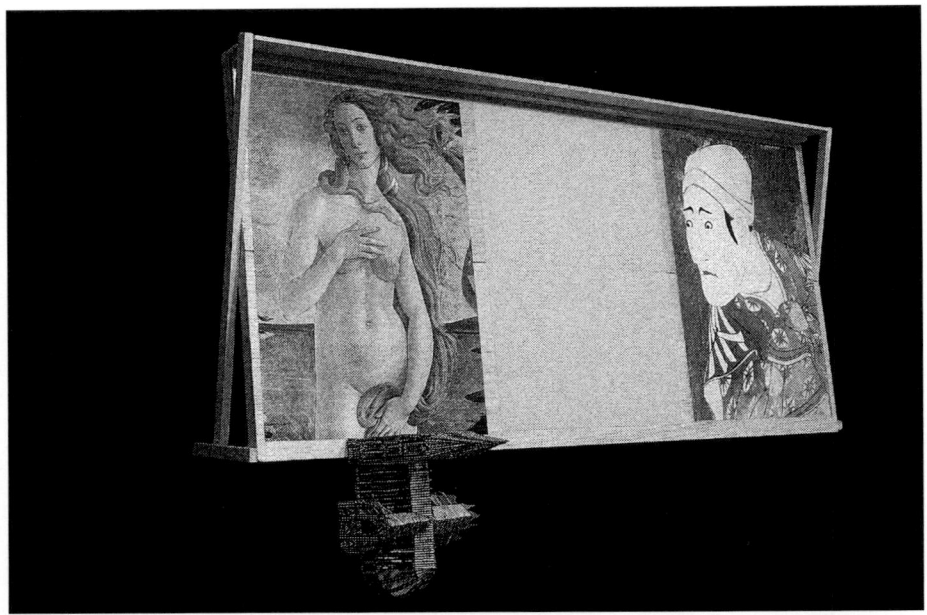

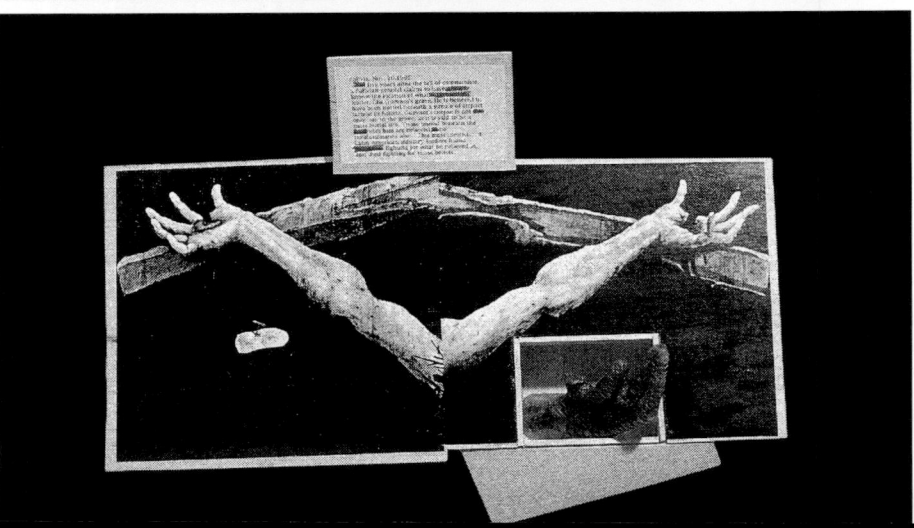

rent issues. These changing realities are vividly expressed in Romberg's recent water colors, which are a development of those that accompanied his earlier architectural works. Now the buildings in the watercolors seem to have become infected with bacteria, which in turn infect other buildings. Architecture ends up as a metaphor for destruction, a destruction for which architects also bear responsibility.

On a more conceptual level, this metaphor of destruction represents Romberg's rejoinder to Postmodernism. Romberg, who considers himself as a survivor of Postmodernism, might agree with Kenneth Frampton's description of postmodernist architecture as the conscious ruination and cannabalism of architectural form.

Yet I think that Romberg hints at another, more positive interpretation of architectural space. It is expressed in the Syzgy series, where he creates an alternative space – a third space which is invested with new meaning. Taking his cue from Gropius, who described the Cathedral of the Future as a place that will once more encompass all the arts in one form as the ideal house, the ideal space. Romberg in this series proposes

I had only one significant teacher, Gaston Breyer. He taught architecture but he really taught vision. He respected his students alot, and was an anarchist; he would ask you to explain what grade you deserved and would then put whatever you told him. He introducd me to Bachelard and to Heidegger – he was an extremely cultured man. His ideas about painting were not mine, but those about philosophy were fantastic.

lover's grasp. Shah Jahan must have known this as he erected his wife's memory. He would have looked across to the black footprint awaiting him, incomplete. The history of architecture would not sanction his dualist lament. As we raised the mast

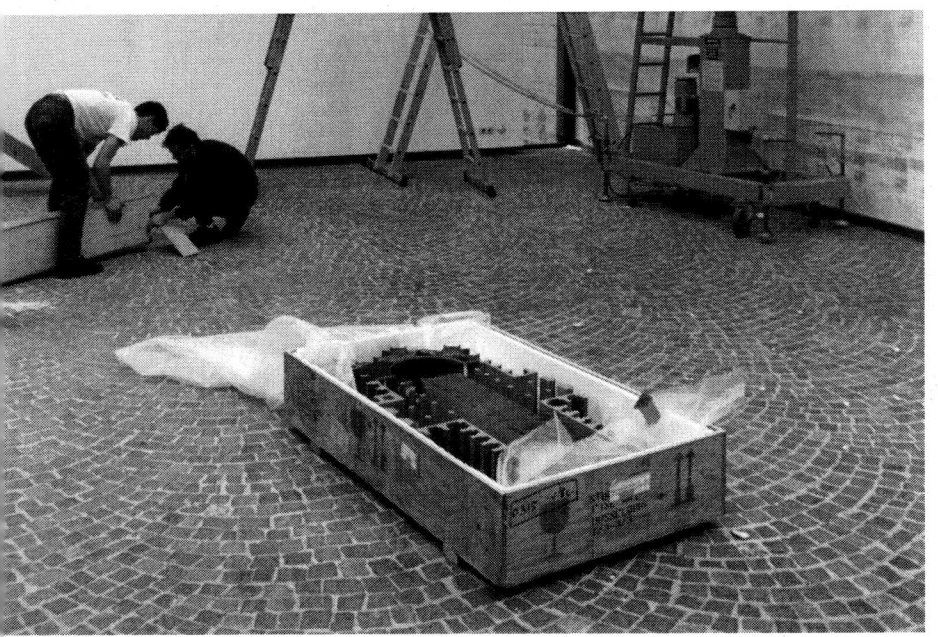

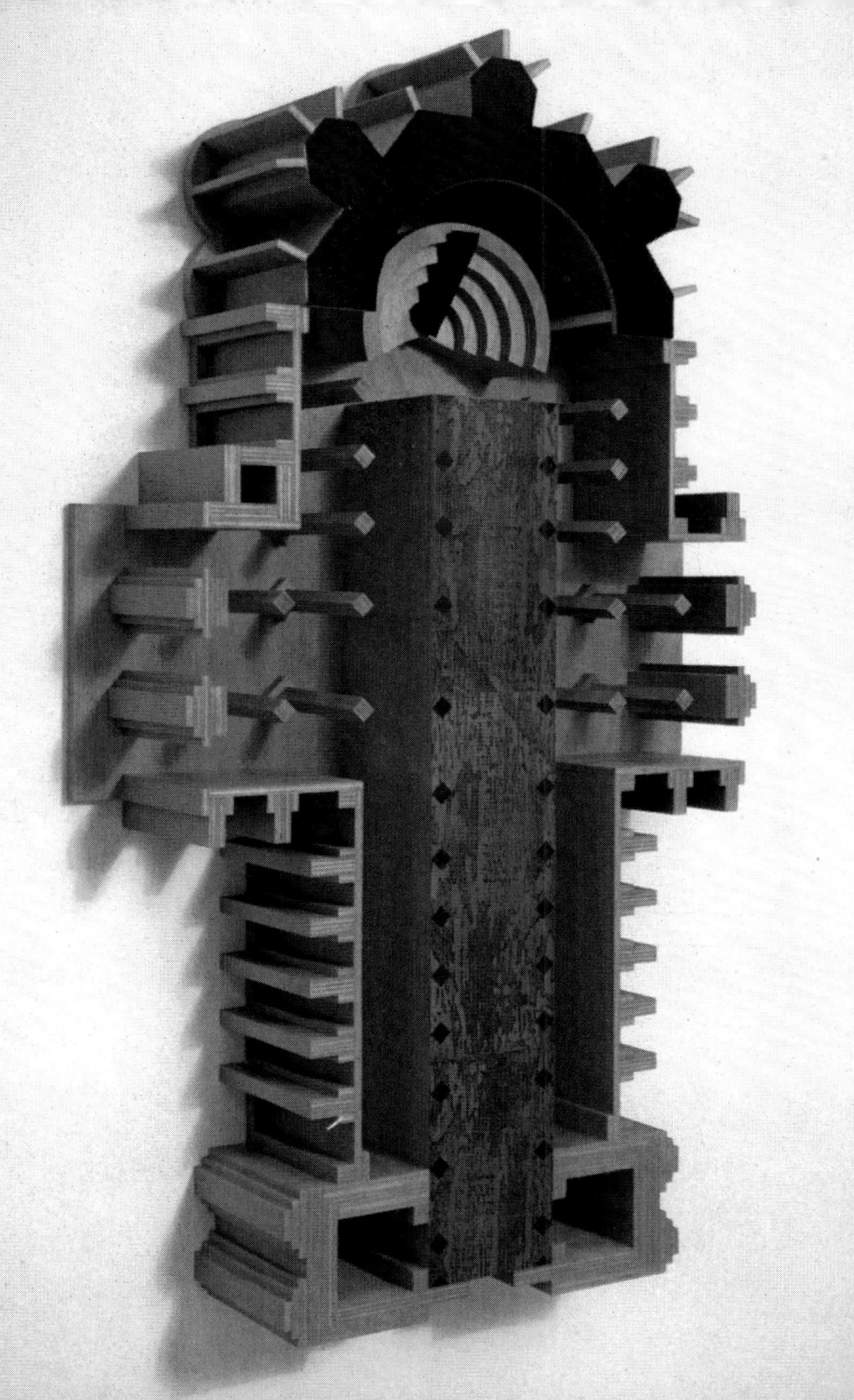

and headed home, I could not help but mutter under my breath: forgive them for they know not what they do. We docked at Pireus, and kept with tradition, seeking ablutions before seeking admiration. Even in glory, there is ritual. The priest went

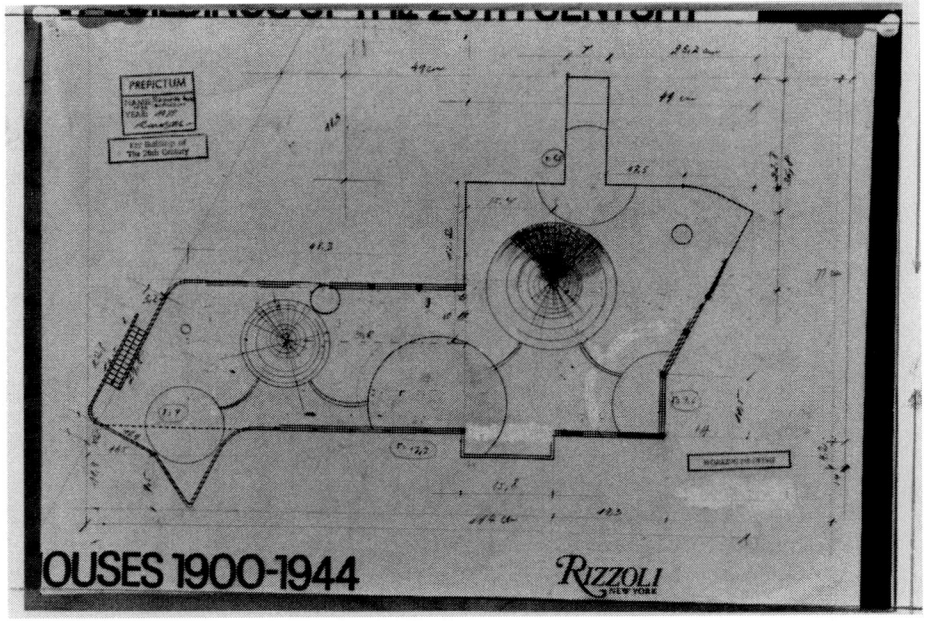

his own Cathedral of the Future. For *Syzgy III*, four temple sites were selected: a Buddhist temple, a Polish Synagogue, an Italian church and an Iranian Mosque. The four building plans overlap in the wall drawing and create a site for meditation. The same space is reproduced in full scale on the floor in front of the wall drawing. People sit and meditate, their eyes resting on a text of Borges which is manipulated to create a subtext that reads as an aphorism. This subspace invested with new meaning can be seen as a "third space," as Edward W. Soja defines it, or "a place, where all places are, an Aleph", as Borges terms it.

For Romberg, it is perhaps a place of renewed spirituality arising from an interdependence of existing cultures and the ashes of extinct ones. This new sphere incorporates and connects all spaces and, like the Aleph, interconnects all art styles and all architecture.

from captain to lookout laying his benevolence flat, irrespective of rank and privilege. His iconography bore the illusion of democracy over a shroud of gold. For whom did we go to the East? Before whose altar did we kneel? What entreaties had we

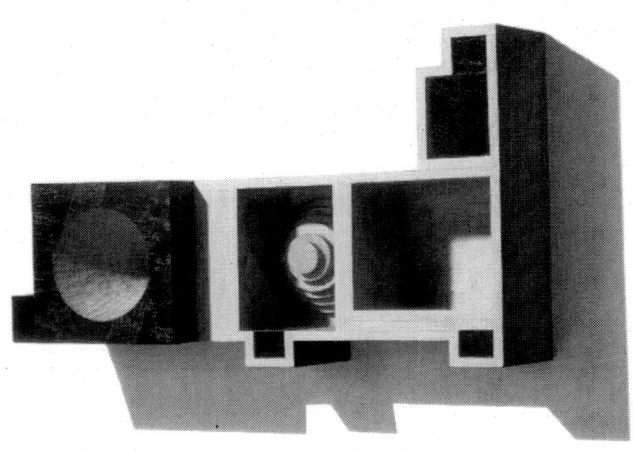

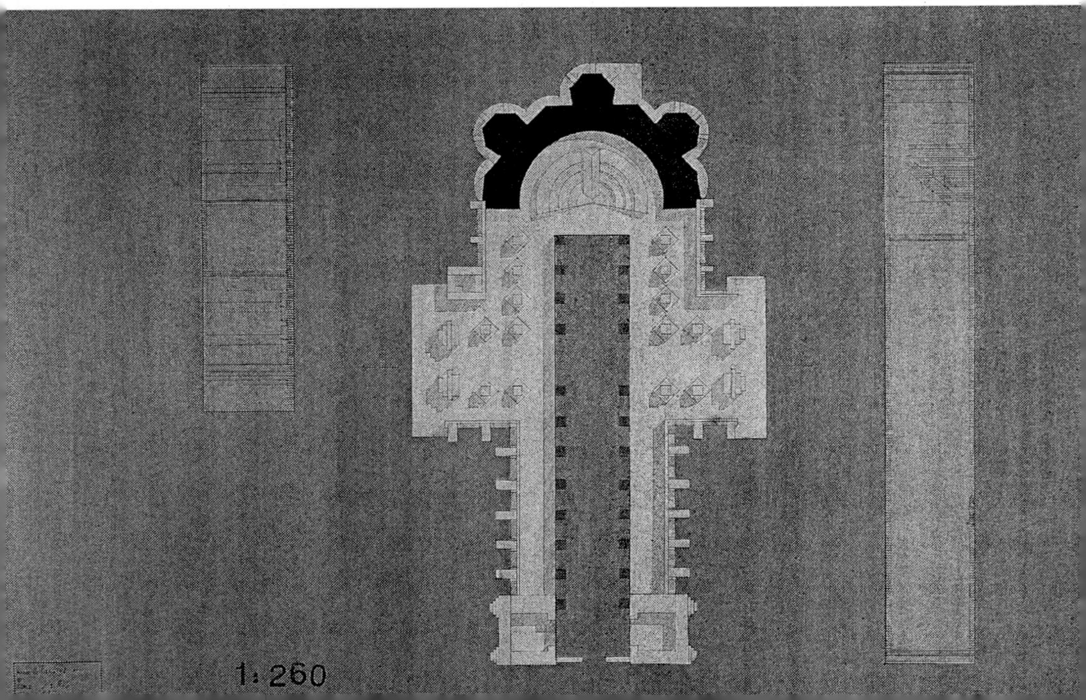

1:260

I found I didn't have any desire to be an architect, to deal with such heavy exterior pressures on creativity.

I have dedicated a large part of my work since the mid-eighties to sensualising the poetics of building footprints. They are the traces of history, and that is why it is related to my permanent preoccupation with the mark of history, with traces, with fossils, with typologies in art and natural science. It's the question of the line between cultural evolution and cultural Darwinism. Sometimes I feel that art belongs more to the natural sciences than to the social sciences.

gained, which entrances did they gain us, and which assignations were now ours? On Sunday, to which chambers would we now be called, and what rooms would lie beyond? On which scale would our pound of flesh be weighed? /// My seventh

art in the nth degree, revisited:
osvaldo romberg and "world space"
ROBERT MAHONEY

I.

Osvaldo Romberg and I have known each other for almost a decade, and we met the way every artist and critic should meet – in a meeting of minds. I reviewed a show he was in at Thread Waxing Space in New York in October, 1993, for Flash Art, he called me up, and said that I had really hit on something in his art, let's talk. Since I owe my participation in today's symposium to that moment, what I wanted to do here was take a walk down memory lane, recreate what was going on in my mind and my criticism at the moment when Romberg's work and my ideas came together, and, I hope, give a sense of what I see in Romberg's work and why it keeps me coming back.

In the late 1980s I had fashioned a critical model of "world space" to inform my writing about public art, how art fits into urban life, how art and architecture go together, and how all contemporary cities keep and remember history, and how

After leaving the Facultad de Arquitectura de Buenos Aires, I didn't see Breyer for many years, as I stopped studying architecture in 1962. Then in 1968 or 1969 I went to be a juror in Tucuman, in the North of Argentina. I did a critique in their salon, and gave a seminar.

voyage ended in strife. It took up the same trajectory as all the others: first an ambulatory passage, second a reverent disembarking, third a consecration (the bodies and the blood), fourth a deliverance. It was only upon return that our charter proved untrue. It would seem that it was not discovery nor mapping that had been in order,

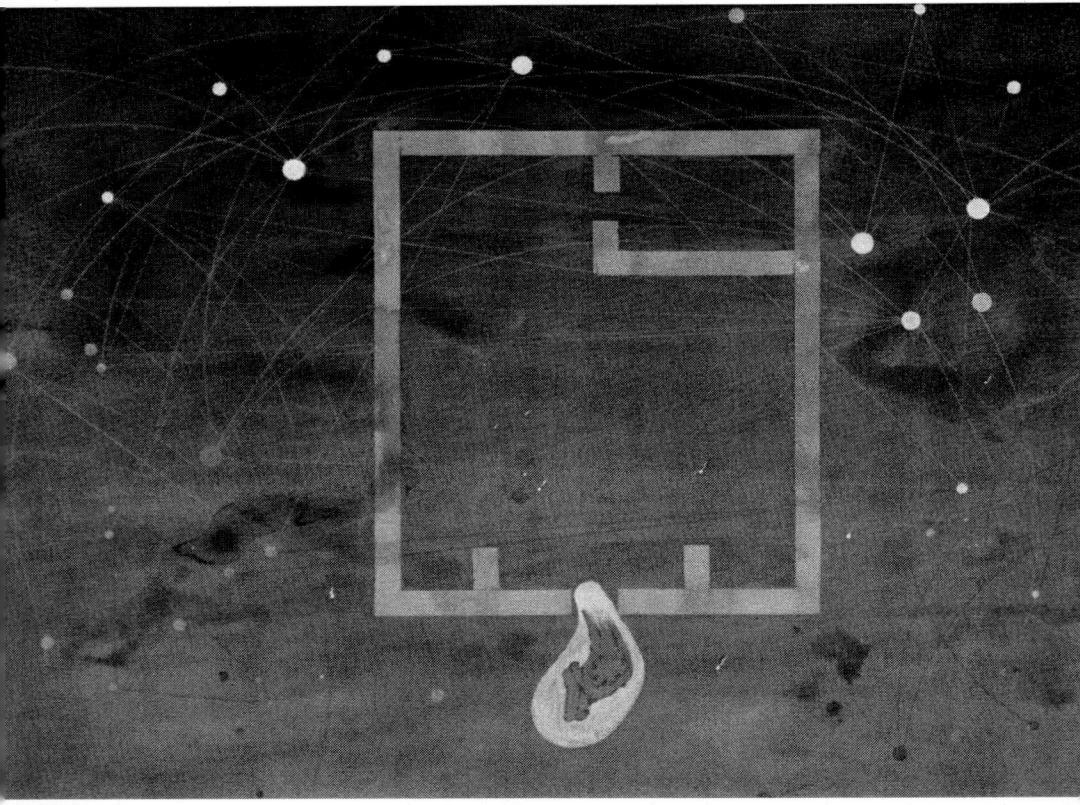

all of these issues serve as a metaphor for how we stand in the time-space continuum of life. I wrote a lot about public art then, and felt strongly that most of it was faltering in its mandate to claim a permanent place in the urban landscape (the dismantling of Richard Serra's "Tilted Arc" remains the Waterloo of permanent public sculpture in America). My model informed much of my enthusiasm for the Velvet Revolution in Eastern Europe in 1989, and fueled an optimism I felt for "neo-conceptual" art in the two to four years following that. Then, as "the new world order" crumbled into a false start, the art world crashed, and fetishism took over, my discourse shifted to a darker place. The work of public art that then seemed to best exemplify what I wanted in sculpture responsive to "world space" in an effective way was Daniel Buren's "Colonnes" in the Palais Royal in Paris. The way that Buren used repetition (columns), abstraction (many of them cut off), transparency (with the spaces below, and the awnings above), and also accommodated the individual (tourists completed the columns by standing on top of them for photos) constituted a major achievement for contemporary art in a historical city center. In my analysis, I sensed that these means of expression somehow evoked all of the his-

They asked me what I thought about the school, what changes I would recommend —at the time it was a typical Argentinian school, with teachers teaching the native style, but art schools can never be perfect.

I needed someone else to help assess the situation, and so I went to visit Breyer. We returned to Tucuman, and Breyer and I taught seminar every week on theory and practice, him the theory and I the practice. It was called "Journeys Into Visual Experience."

but claims to structure, sovereignty, stardom and order itself. It was not enough to unroll the vellum over Terra Australis, something had to be caught in its net. Their designs were not the first to fail, they had chased their own tales only to become a rat-king. Civilization's expansive architecture became an imperial prosthesis, an

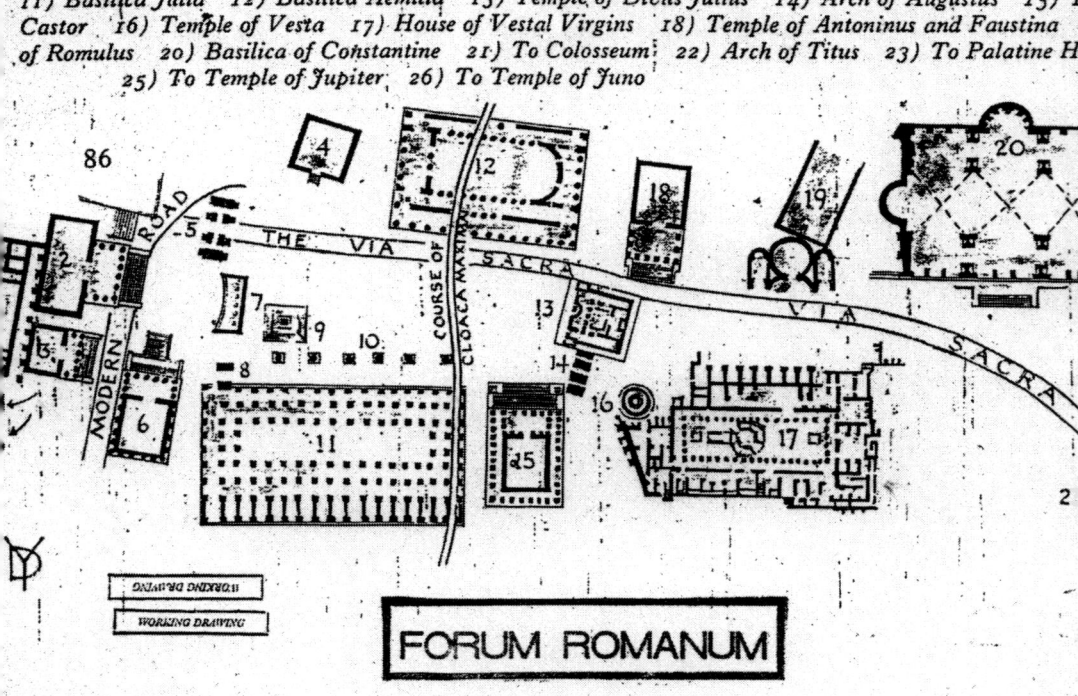

Forum Romanum (reconstruction) looking towards Capitol Hill.
1) Tabularium   2) Temple of Concord   3) Temple of Vespasian   4) Curia   5) Arch of Septimius S
6) Temple of Saturn   7) Imperial Rostra   8) Arch of Tiberius   9) Column of Phocas   10) Honorar
11) Basilica Julia   12) Basilica Aemilia   13) Temple of Divus Julius   14) Arch of Augustus   15) T
Castor   16) Temple of Vesta   17) House of Vestal Virgins   18) Temple of Antoninus and Faustina
of Romulus   20) Basilica of Constantine   21) To Colosseum   22) Arch of Titus   23) To Palatine H
25) To Temple of Jupiter   26) To Temple of Juno

FORUM ROMANUM

tory that had occurred in the colonnade around the Palais Royal (it was where in 1789 the riot that began the revolution was incited, etc.), and yet it did so without historicism or antiquarianism, creating a porous, resonant field of echoing forms which evoked a sense of the past in the present.

Buren, then, was the model for how an artist should abstractly evoke two centuries of history in a haunted contemporary site. But Paris had more to offer my thinking. After leaving the Palais Royal, having completed my "review" of Buren's work, I came out into the Place de la Comédie Francaise. I thought my work was done. But when I crossed the street, I saw a small plaque on the facade above the opening of a Japanese restaurant which said that on this spot, Joan of Arc was burned at the stake in 1345. I had formulated a model of urban time-space continuum with a depth of two or, at the most, three centuries of echoes. My American myopia was obviously showing, and why not? Most American cities were founded in the 1830s, rebuilt in 1900-1920, and rebuilt again after World War II. For me (a Midwesterner), New York City, with echoes of the 17th and 18th centuries, was the "old country." Up to then I was think-

The biggest influence in art academies today are ArtForum, magazines and the market and less so the teachers t hemselves. Most schools are provincial, a core of teachers who are artists by chance; they don't know what they're doing. Even visiting artists who inspire through their success and skill don't become full time teachers – the veneer might slip off, it would be too dangerous.

92 | *arbitrary knot of hysteria and ennui, planted between mere form and desired func-*
tion. To the benign indifference of the universe, I would not lay my heart open. My
first pirate voyage was bathed in its precursors' tired metaphor: the Defiant and its
crew would cleave the seas in two. In our naivety we compressed the navy's vertical

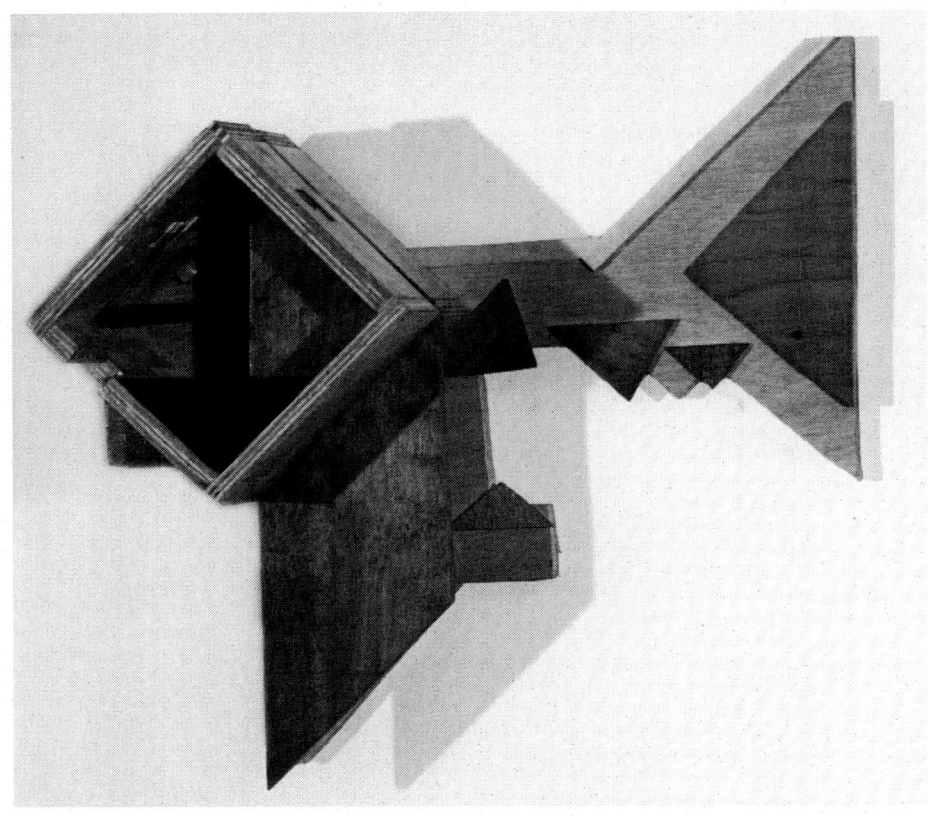

ing I could measure the resonance of the time-space continuum in degrees – first degree, second degree, third degree, something like that – based on how far back the site went. Now I realized that the degrees can go so far back that they merge, for the mind in the present, into an unabsorbable abstraction. That degree where a calculable sense of time in experience disappears into an abstract, "legendary" and "tradition"-oriented sense of time, I term the nth degree.

A time-space continuum of the nth degree is a honeycomb-like "tradition," an upside down chandelier - part fact, part fiction, part history, part superstition, a common sense half-forgetful comprehension of the past as the shadowed part of the present. When the time-space continuum runs to the nth degree, it creates a highly abstract, ethereal zone reverberating with countless timelines, and that space I call "World Space." An architect, sculptor or artist, can only adequately respond to the complexity of life today by building or creating in such a "tradition," with a deep awareness of the continuum. My thinking at the time focused on city centers in world capitals: more particularly, I further described world space, in an almost economic way, as an upside down chandelier complex-ity of spatial arrangements which develop especially in the world center of any particular market, economy or culture: "Whenever a city becomes a capital, the prior arrangement of fields falls in under the umbrella of world culture. You often have redundant developments of fields under new specialized world conventions, framing and enclosing, literally re-contextualizing space." This continuous process over centuries leads to a high degree of spatial repetition and transparency ..."contributing to the richness of the parallax effect of its space and the spectacle it induces."

As a simple, graphic and utilitarian critical tool, the idea of "world space" gave me a set of of criteria by which to judge a work of public art: good public art responded to the time-space continuum in an effective manner (my æsthetic then called for a kind of deconstructive abstraction); bad public art ignored the continuum and assisted developers and others in imposing a blocked and obstructive "everything is present" present over the continuum. A work of art, in short, had to have that nth degree in it.

In addition to offering this intellectual model, I also allowed the feelings of the individuals and tourists to enter the pic-

organization into the plain democracy of the sea. As a redistributed mobile whole, our violations were cuts away from the politics of linear borders. Our vision was one of so many cuts, a patchwork of ecstatic fragmentation. Our shredded clothes and flags defied the hegemony of Westphalia and the soft facts of its legal underbelly.

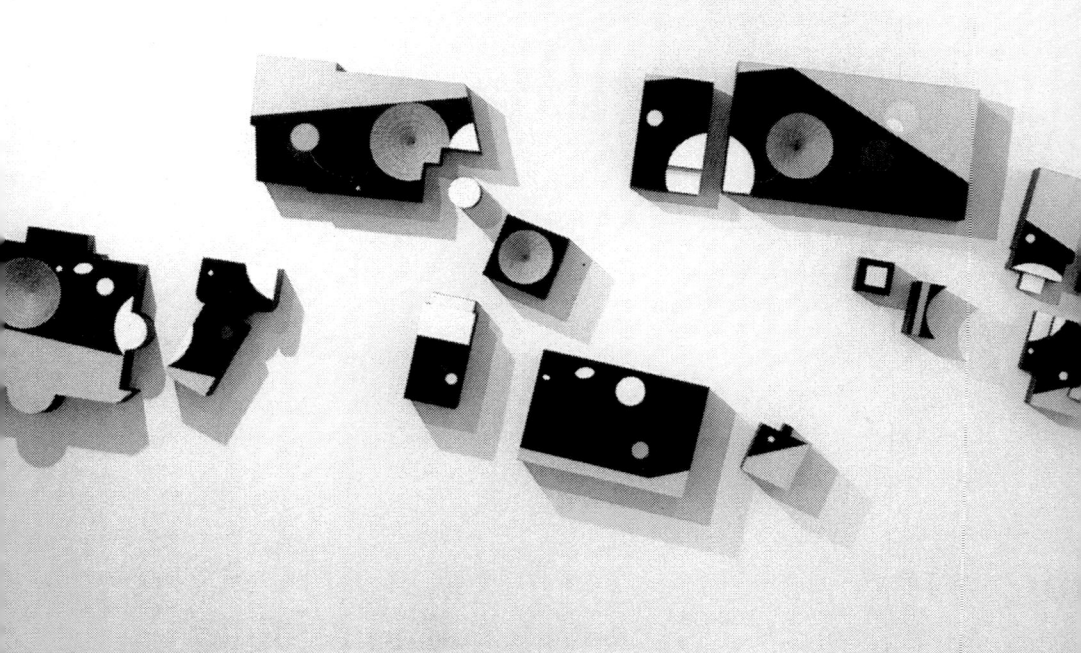

ture. The comprehension of world space always starts with the high or low feelings of a sole individual moved to consider his or her part in the wide world. Traveling is as much about feelings as about seeing the sights. If it happens that an individual feels at one with the depth of time-space at a great sight, a euphoria, a humming joy to be alive, a speechless "I can't believe I am here, and part of this world culture" feeling overcomes one: I call that high a "concordance." But if it gets to be too much, world culture can touch off a depressive episode. The depression associated with exposure to the world I call "abandon," a kind of panic and even agoraphobia.

Most tourists are indeed overwhelmed, but always euphemistically describe their feelings as "a little disappointed" when they visit world sights. Some tourists will try to have a thought of their own about a world sight. But most tourists deny the discomfort of this struggle in an instant pleasurable release: picking up a souvenir, a bit of kitsch to block out the discomfort and make it all digestible and easy again. That's why souvenir stands exist: they offer instant balm to the eternally "a little disappointed." Paris, which more than any other city is a world capital beset by little disappointments, is filled

with postcards to accommodate the downside of monumentality. You can literally take Paris home with you: reliving concordance, soothing abandon, yet, still, somehow, part of the continuum.

2.

I already knew that Osvaldo Romberg was one of the few artists dealing in a rarified way with art at the intersection of architecture, and his Footprints series attests to that. I thought of him as a kind of sculptor, and a maker of public art, his work then within the purview of my critical interest. But here I focus on the collage works exhibited at Thread Waxing Space in 1993 and the particular "time-space continuum" in which I first experienced them.

The exhibition at Thread Waxing Space, "Gone Beyond Gone," was curated by Dominique Nahas (September 18 – October 23, 1993), with work by Osvaldo Romberg. Romberg included, among other pieces, *Looking Anxiously for Sassetta*, 1993, *The Cage*, 1993, and *The Peacock*, 1993. This body of work, all constructed with PVC, balsa wood, transparent tape, lance pins, color reproductions, and collage, featured small reproductions of old master paintings, framed by transparent

A flotilla of alternate blueprints lay always already in wait for its bricoleur. But as Empire's outposts stretched to envelope us, our plans refused classification. The pages of pirate utopia resist their ledgers, preferring to be found in the labyrinths of collective imagination.

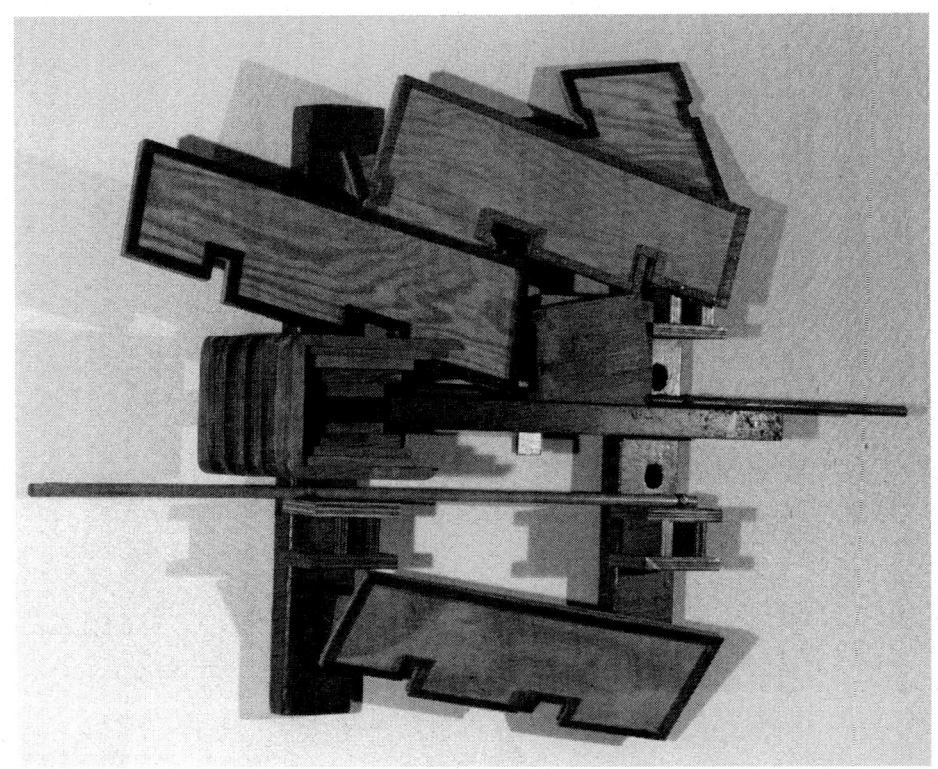

enclosures, and – this immediately hit the spot – imposed upon by tiny postcard cutouts of monuments of architecture.

Only a few times in a career do a critic's thoughts and obsessions merge and commune with an artist's. This was one of those moments. I had long since been examining how reproduction and reality mix in the "tradition" of a world space: Romberg used primarily art history book reproductions in his work. I was exploring repetition and transparency as a way to express world space: Romberg is all repetition of form and transparency in material. I was also exploring how the individual feels in that space, and often, in weak moments, uses kitsch representations such as postcards as balm to manage life in that space. Romberg was using precisely these little architectural postcards.

Moreover, Romberg's imagery featured the theme of how great art exists in the world, as the real thing or as reproduction, and whether it even matters any more. Romberg's PVC plastic enclosures reminded me of the world space that can form around an icon, such as the glass box which the "Mona Lisa" was then trapped in: a glass box reflecting

I like America. I can have a couple of beers without working very hard. In Paris, you have to kill someone to get a steak. Beer here costs thirty cents. I like the naïveté you find in America: they say anything is possible, and you really believe it. Yet I don't think I'll live in America for too many more years.

I like Sarkozy. He's a dandy. The socialists don't do anything. Mitterand was a nice guy, but he was only good for painting with his legislative protectionism towards French galleries.

camera flash glare in a way that ironically makes it difficult to see the painting itself. Romberg's boxy, bubbling enclosures, altering perspectives, also made me think about the tourist fetish for the "Mona Lisa" and how it caused every other painting in the gallery (many major works by major painters) to be utterly ignored (in Europe, time and again, masterpieces are placed in out of the way places: since Watteau's "Voyage to Cythera" was placed too near to an entrance to the Grand Salon, and is rushed past by hoards of tourists bee-lining it to "Mona Lisa," it has to remain one of the great underseen masterpieces of Western history).

Romberg's lance pins represented the flimsiness of the "museum without walls" that the individual constructs in his mind. Romberg's use of the architectural postcards (as well as all other do-it-yourself low-tech materials, evocative of private worlds) undoubtedly inverted the art and architectural themes he had been exploring in his *Footprints* series. They telescopically zoom-lensed the space around the painting, and represented the idea of missing, or not seeing, or being just "a little bit disappointed," in front of a masterpiece endowed with the nth degree in world space: in short,

the place of the individual in the world of the nth degree.

It doesn't get much better than that. I wrote a review without hesitation. That short review is one of my most succinct published statements about "world space." When it came out in January, 1994, Romberg called me up, and we've had an ongoing artist-critic dialogue ever since. Both of us have moved onto other issues, but, as you can see, that moment lives on.

INTER
MEZZO

DOUBLE AGENDA

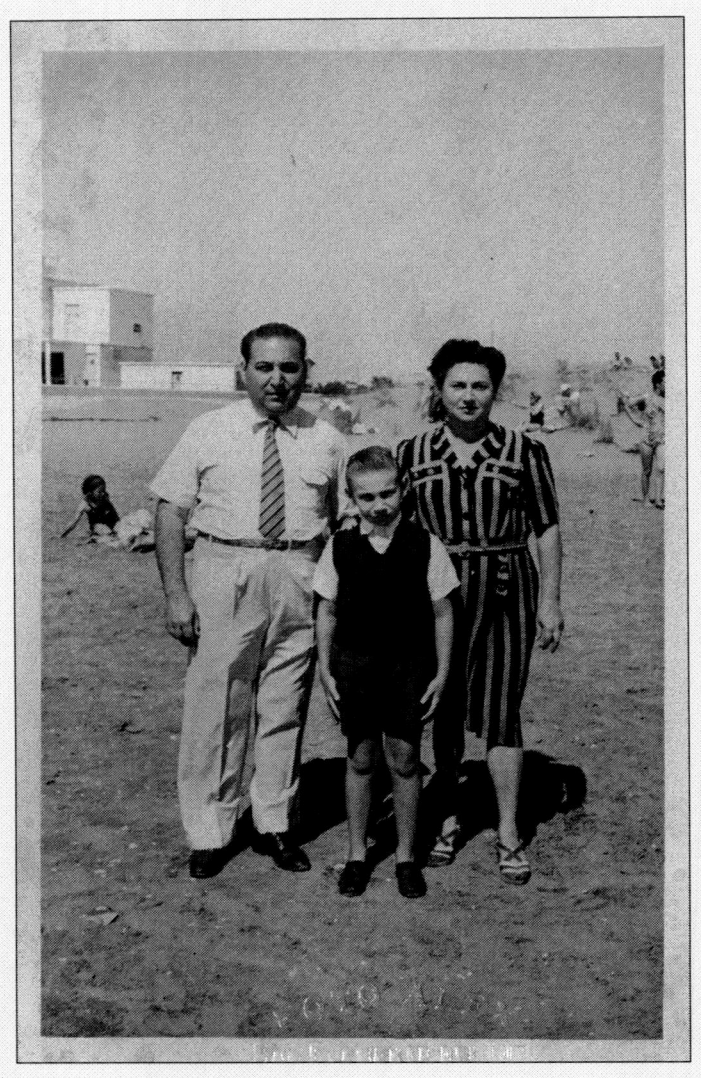

With mother and father
San Clemente, Argentina, circa 1946

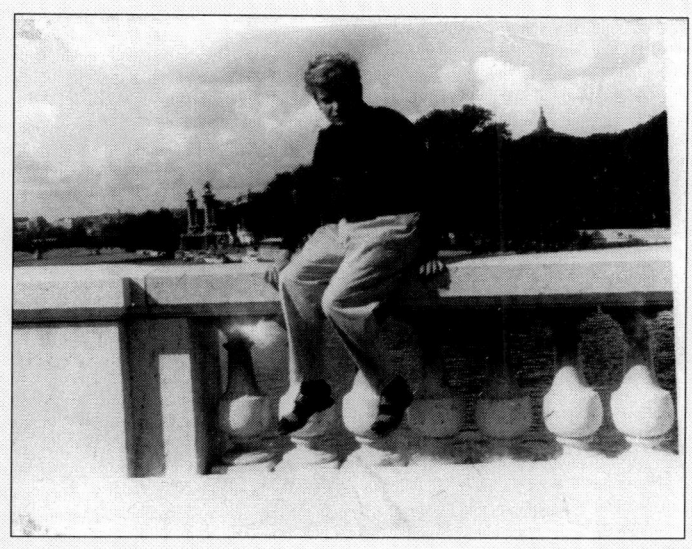

Paris, 1958

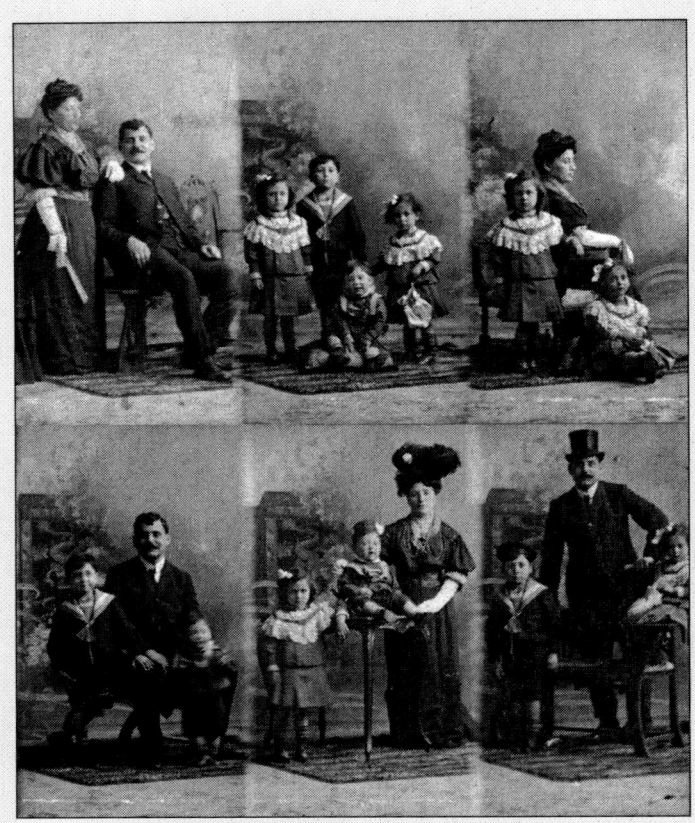

Grandfather, grandmother and uncles
Russia, circa 1908

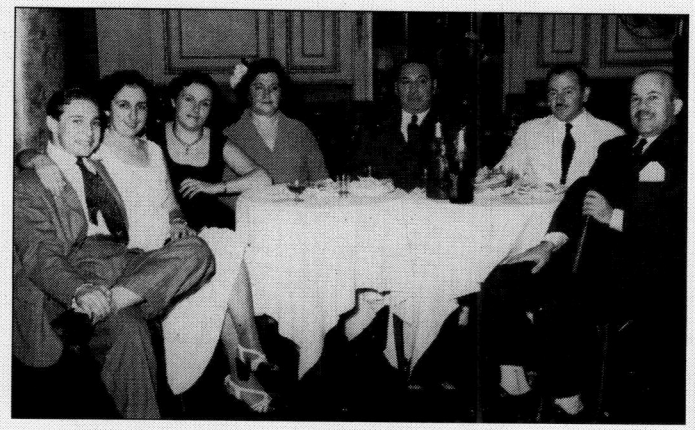

With sisters Chola and Regina, mother and father, brothers-in-law Simon and José,
Buenos Aires, circa 1958

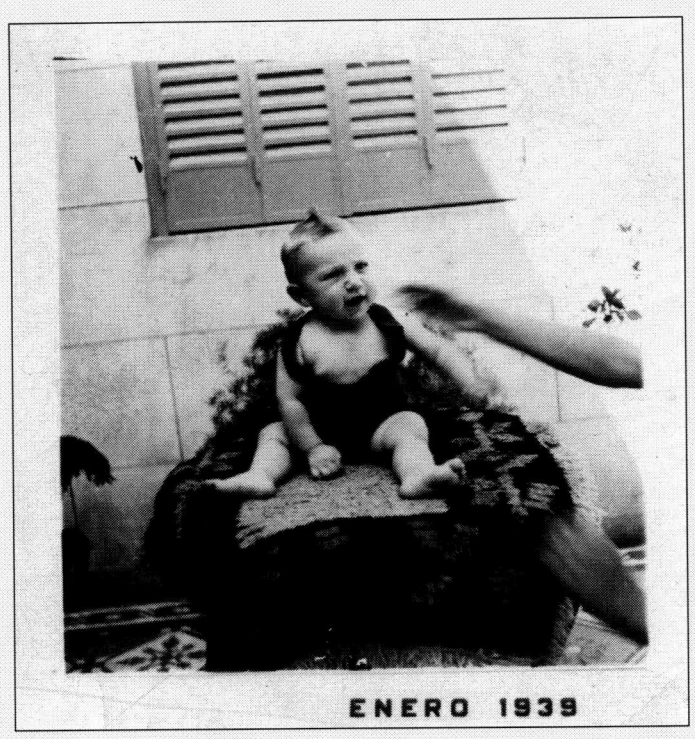

ENERO 1939

Buenos Aires, January 1939

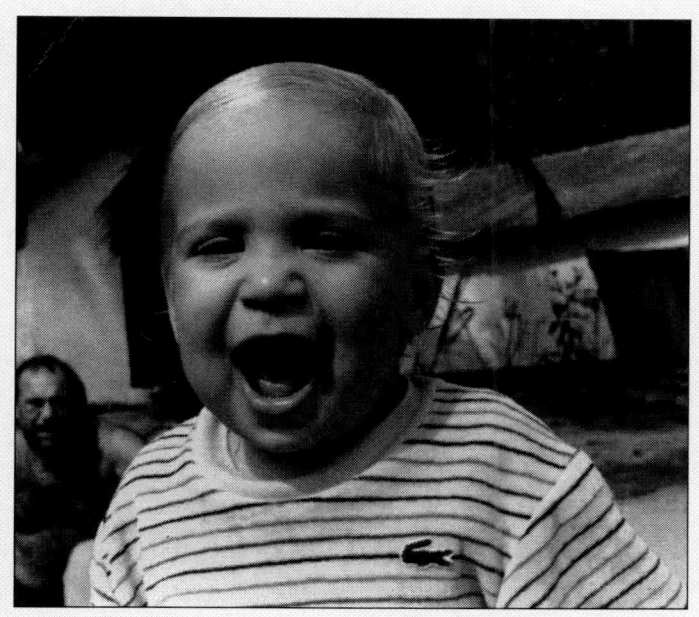

With son David
Isla Grande Brazil, circa 1985

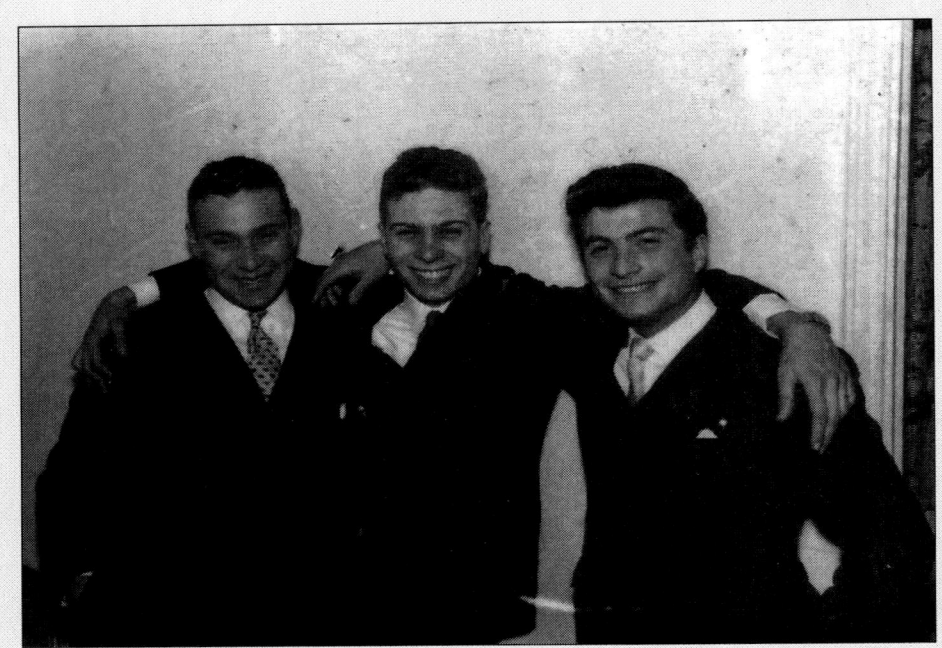

With his cousins Jorge Bercon and Enrique
Berlin, circa 1956

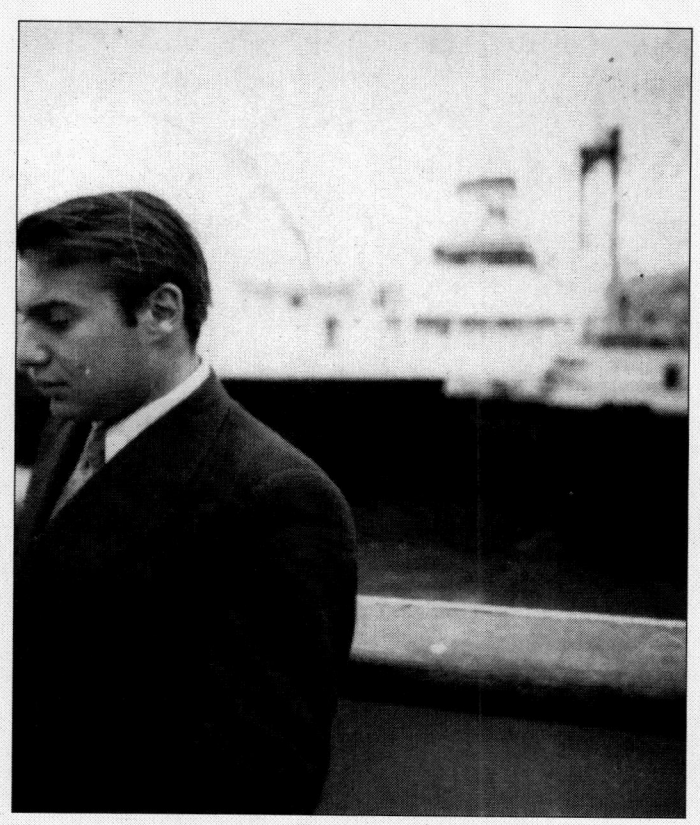

Leaving Argentina for Europe
Aboard the Conte Biancamano, circa 1957

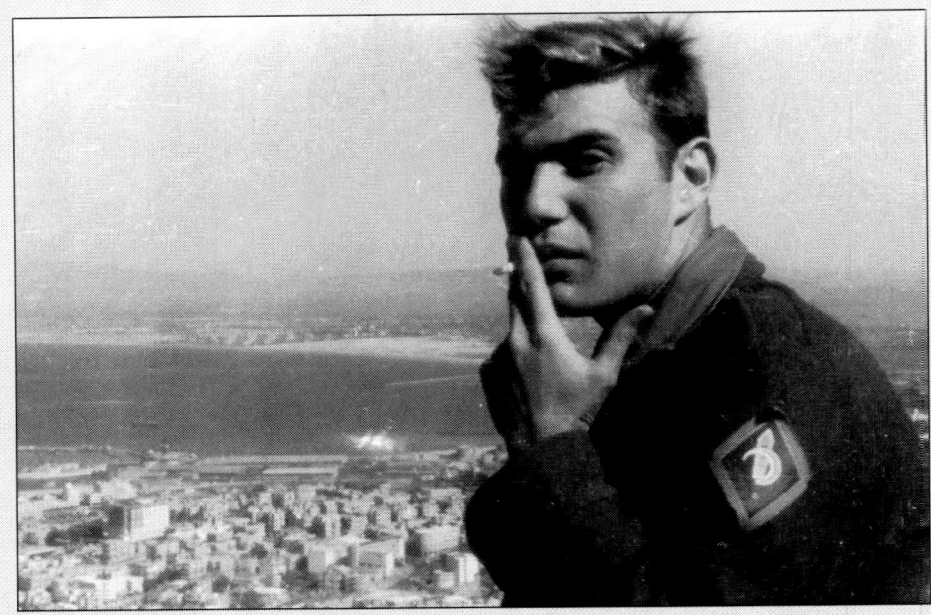

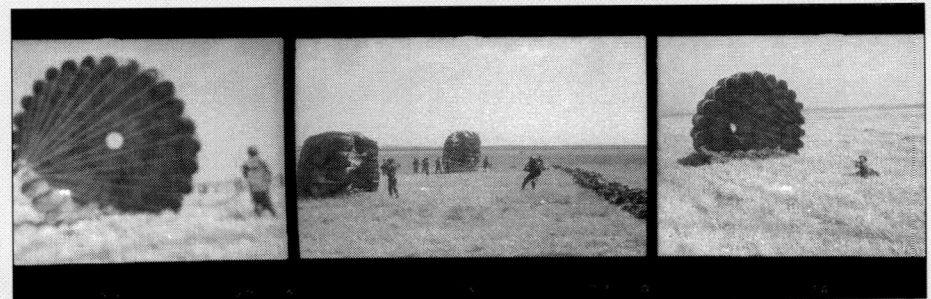

Israel, 1957

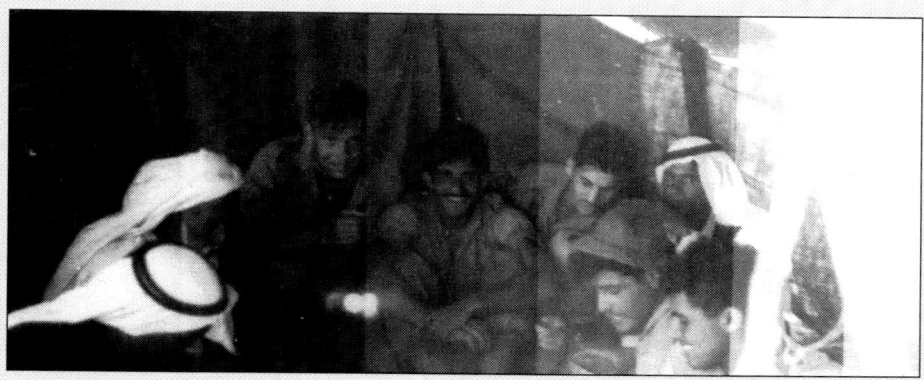

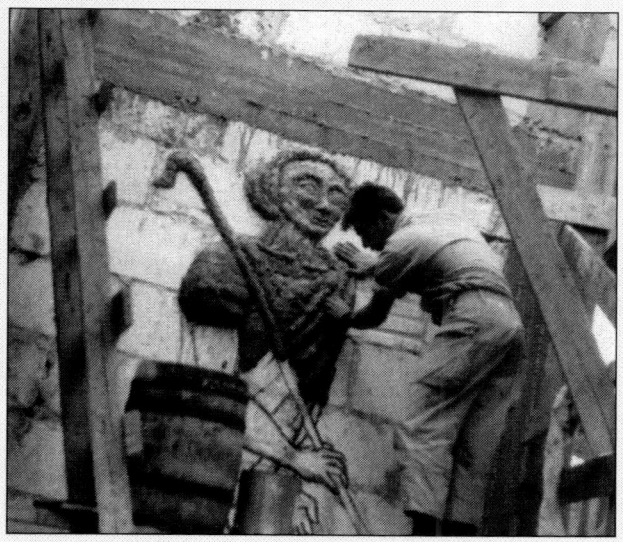

Top: Negev Desert Israel 1958
Bottom: Kibbutz Kfar Szold, 1957

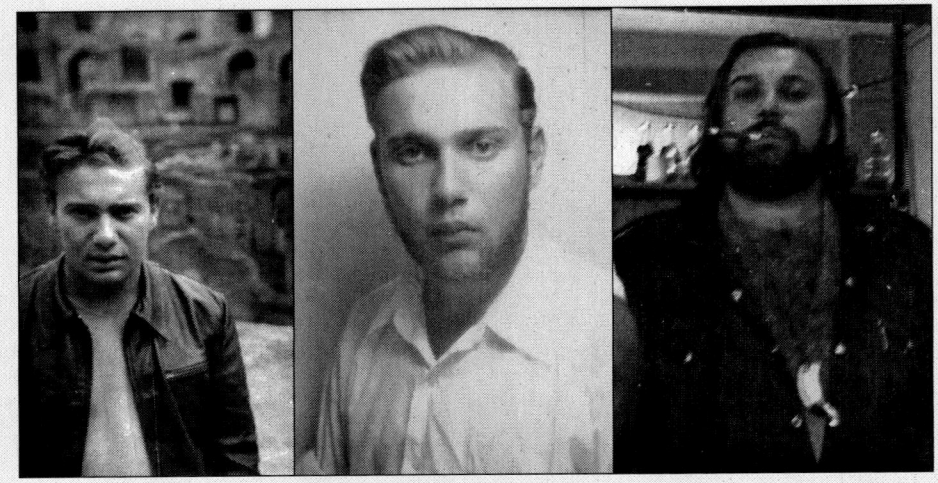

Left: The Coliseum, Rome, 1957
Middle: Tel Aviv, 1957
Right: The College for Arts' Teachers, Herzlia, 1973

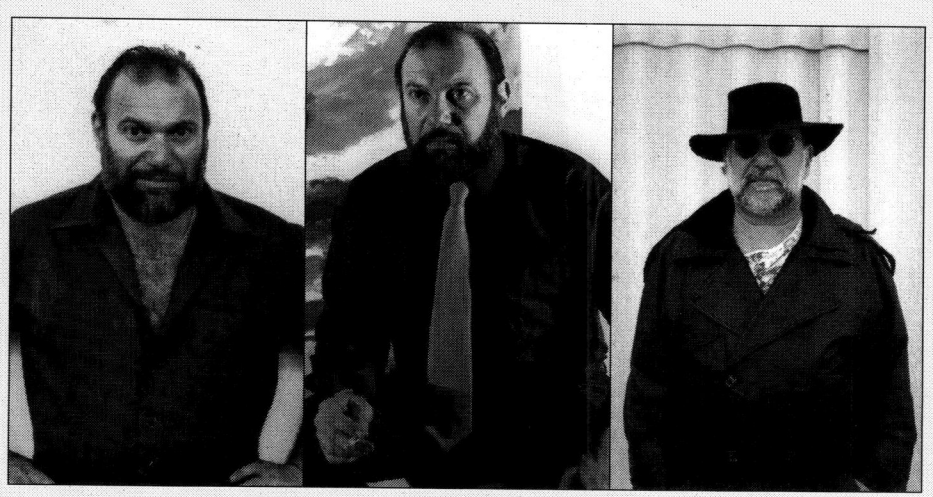

Left: New York Studio, 1982
Middle: New York Studio, 1993
Right: At the Negev, Israel, 1997

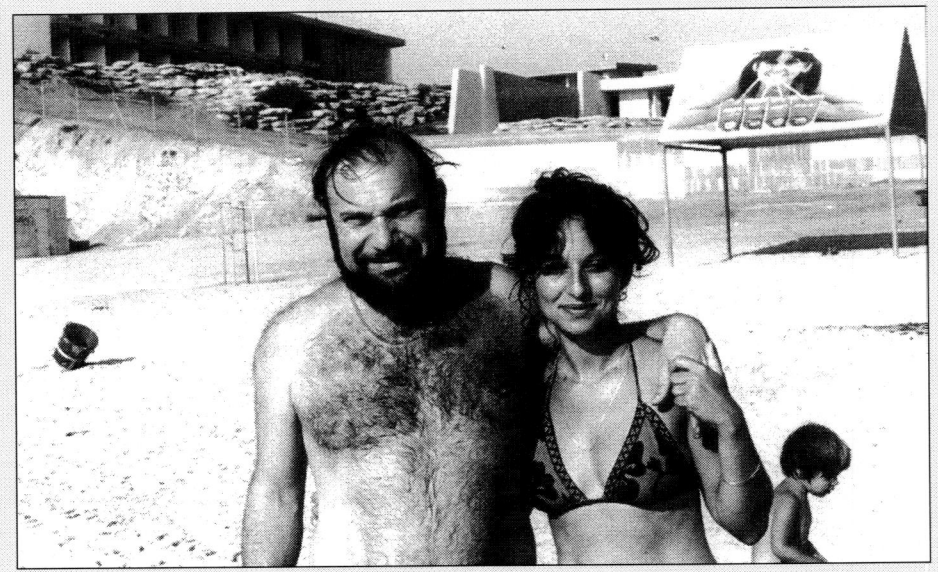

O.R. & Raquel
Herzlya Beach, Israel, circa 1979

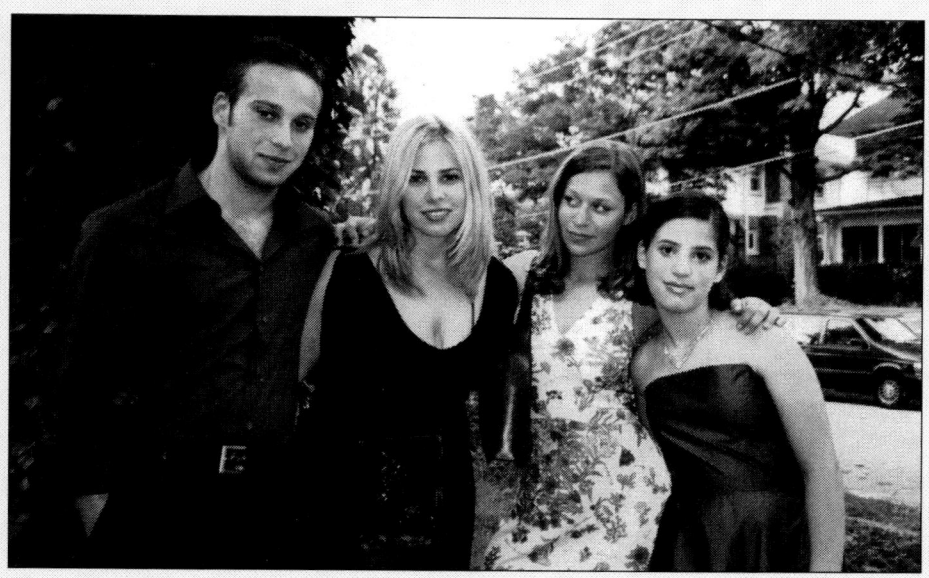

Children: David, Joanna, Noa & Victoria
Philadelphia, 2006

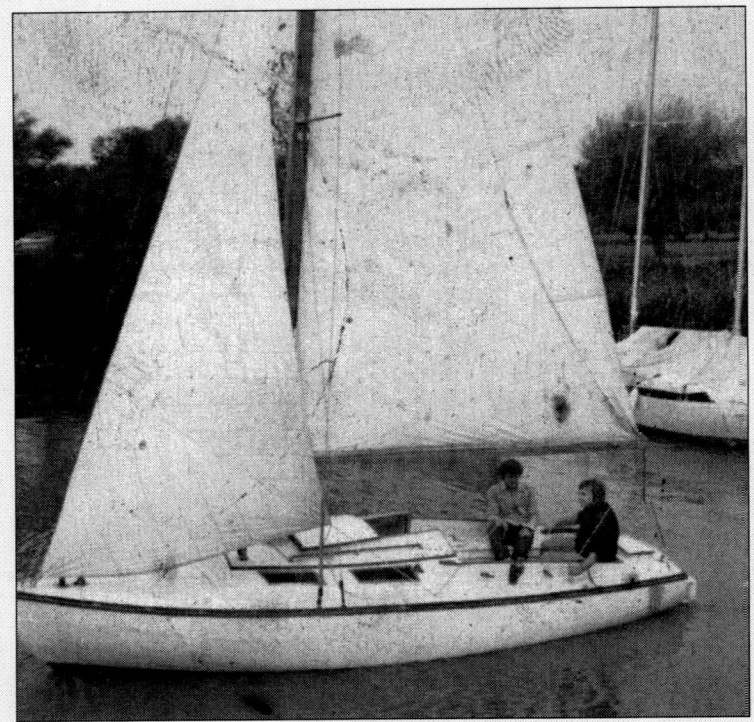

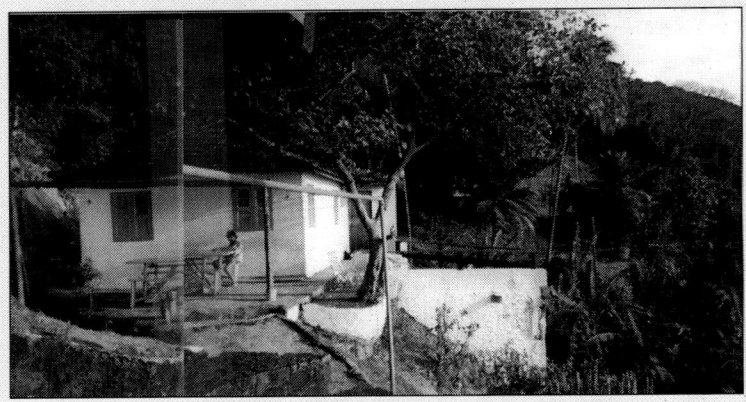

Top: Sailing the Squalus, Rio de la Plata, 1969
Bottom: The island house, Isla Grande, Brazil

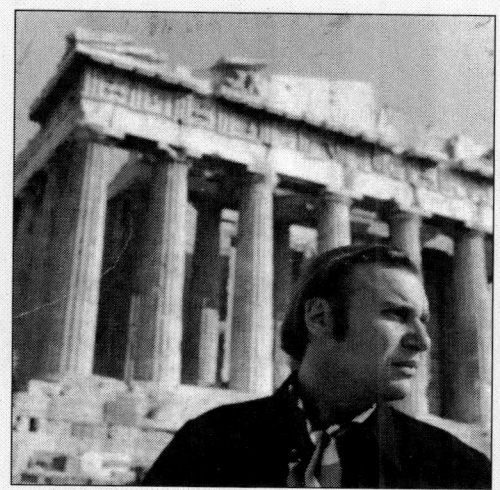

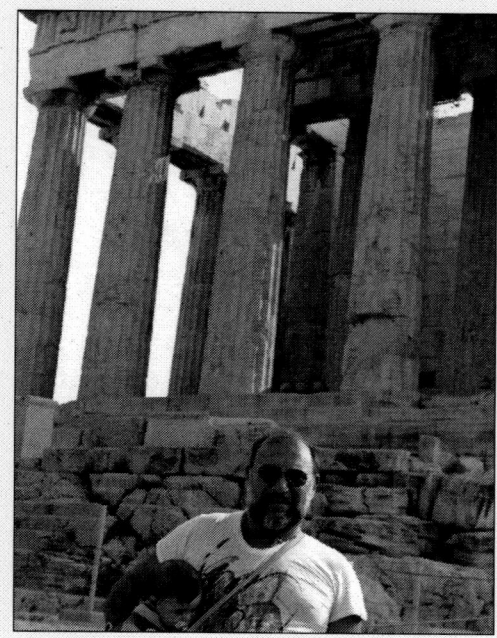

Top: Parthenon, Greece, circa 1968
Bottom: With daughter Victoria, Parthenon, 1989

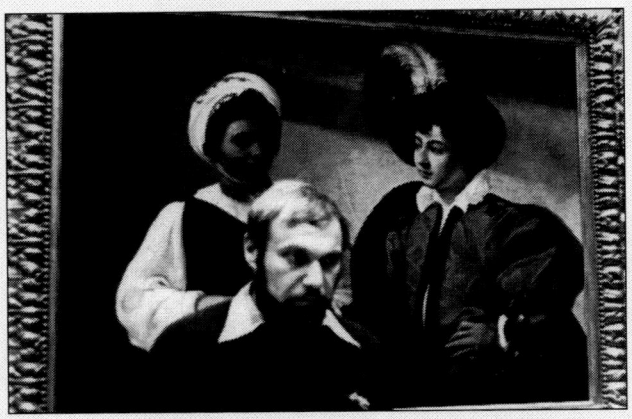

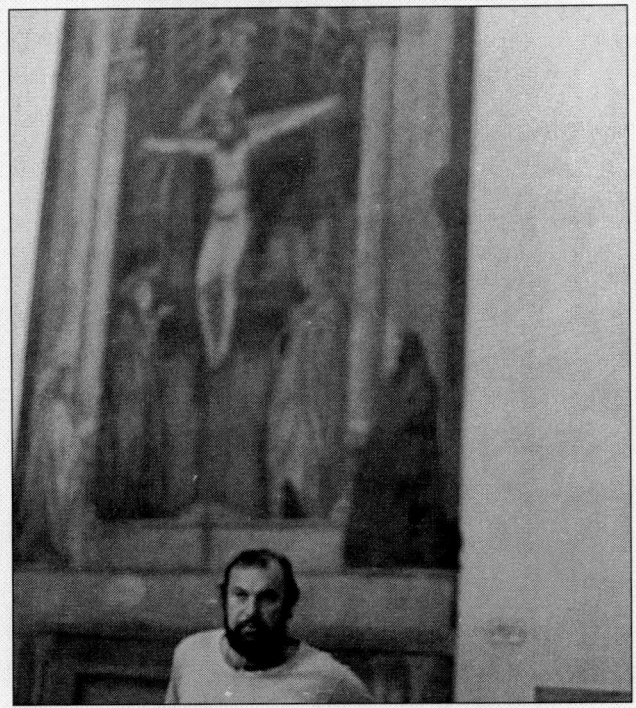

Top: Le Louvre, Paris, circa 1977
Bottom: Basilica di San Francesco in Arezzo, 1978

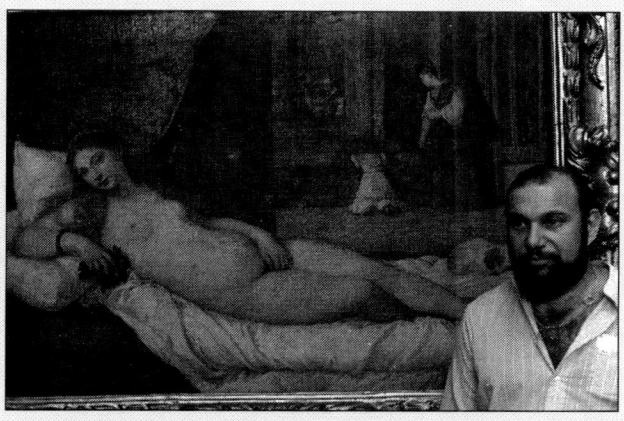

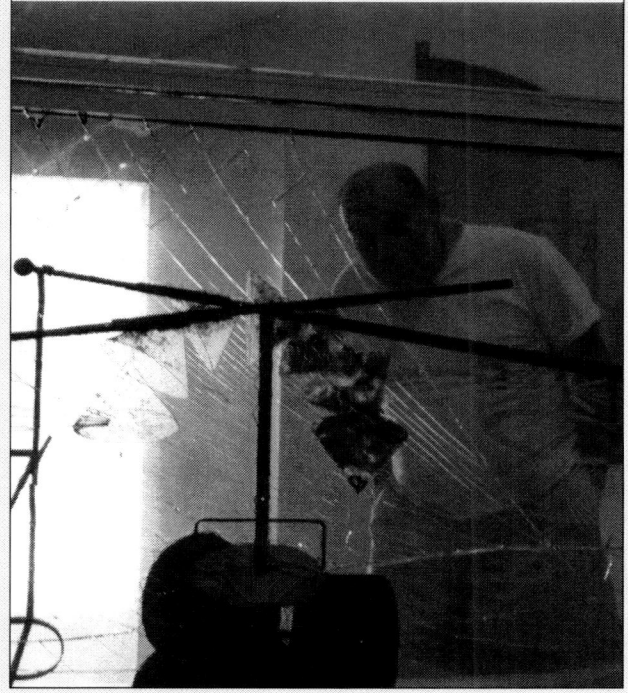

Top: Prado, Madrid, circa 1979
Bottom: Philadelphia Museum of Art, 1993

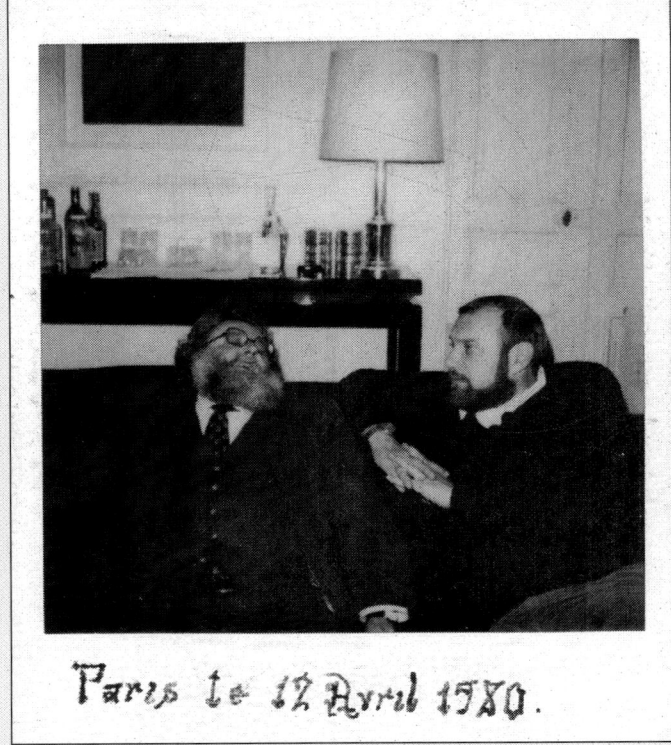

Paris le 12 Avril 1980.

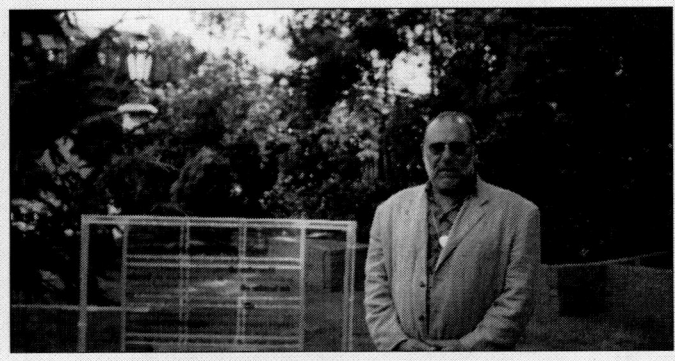

Top: O.R. & Pierre Restany, Paris, 1980
Bottom: Venice Biennale, 1995

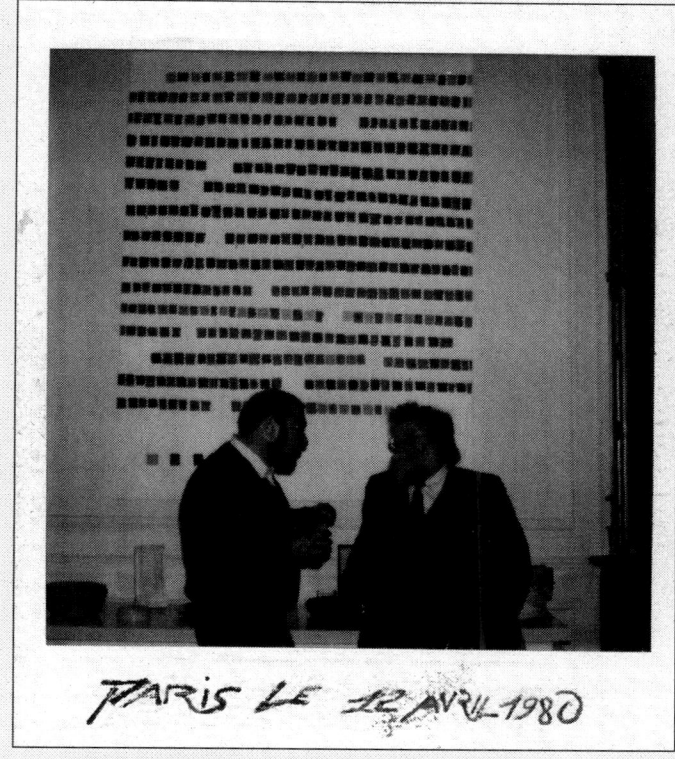

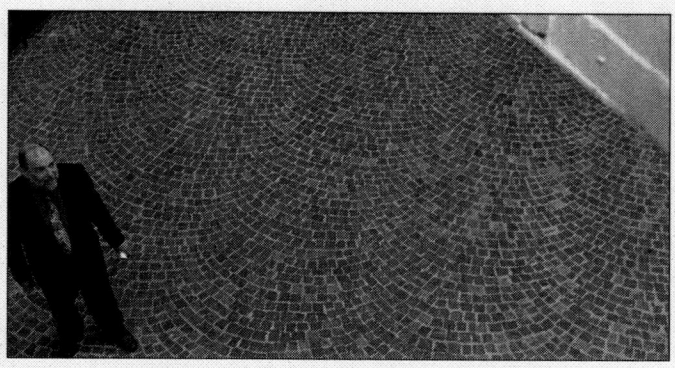

Top: O.R. & Pierre Restany, Paris, 1980
Bottom: Posing as Tatlin, Hanover, 1991

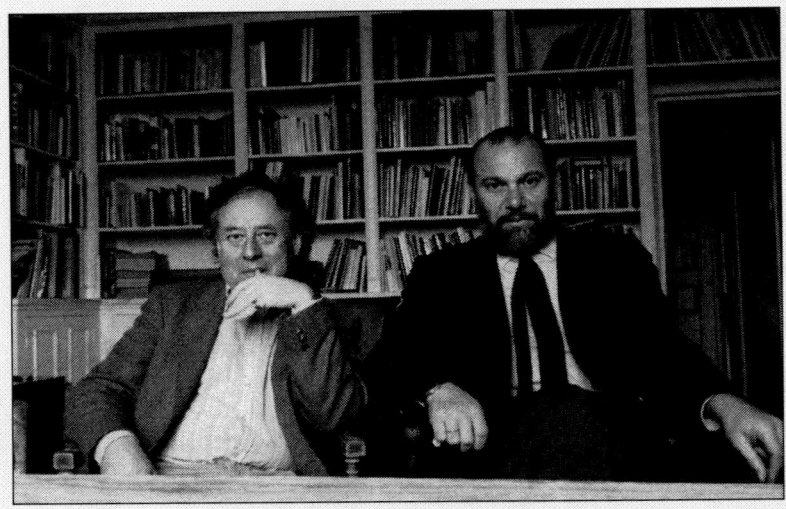

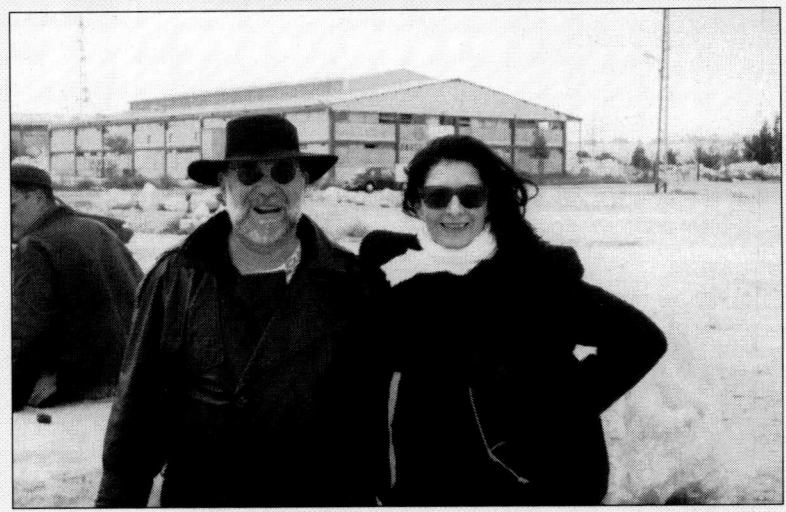

Top: O.R. & Edward Lucy Smith, London, c. 1983
Bottom: O.R & Maria Abramovic, Negev Desert, 1995

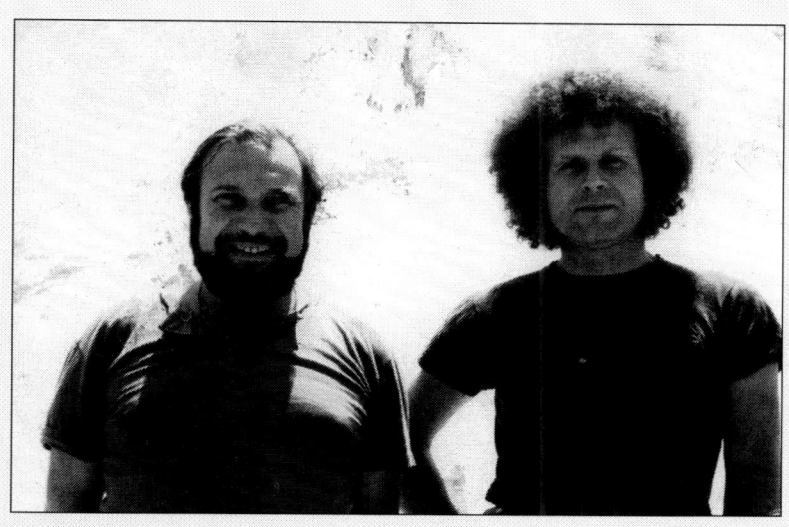

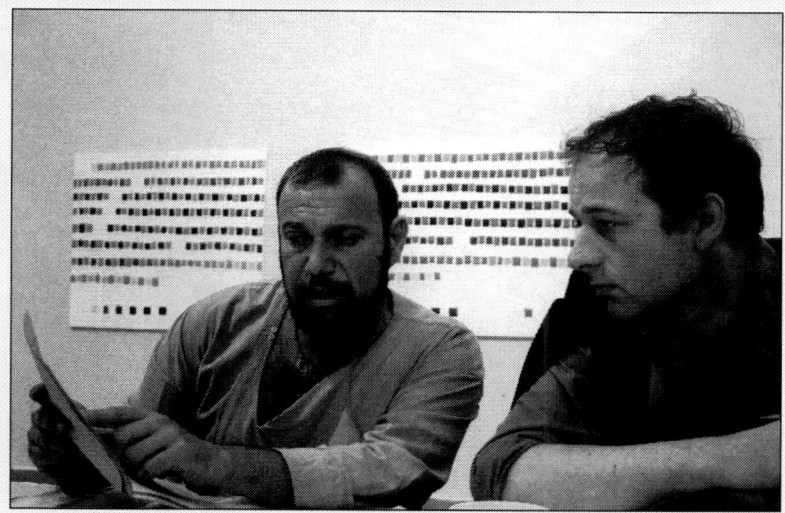

Top: O.R. & Klaus Rinke, Israel, 1978
Bottom: O.R. & Dr. Dieter Ronte, Bonn, 1979

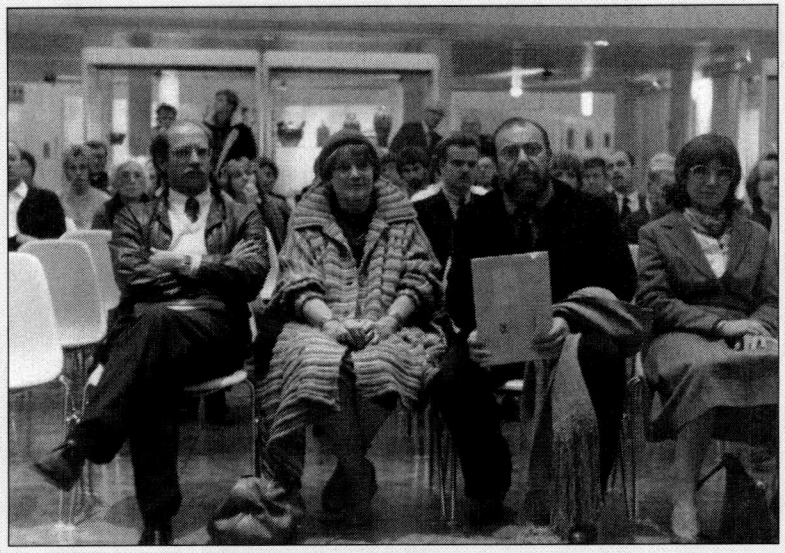

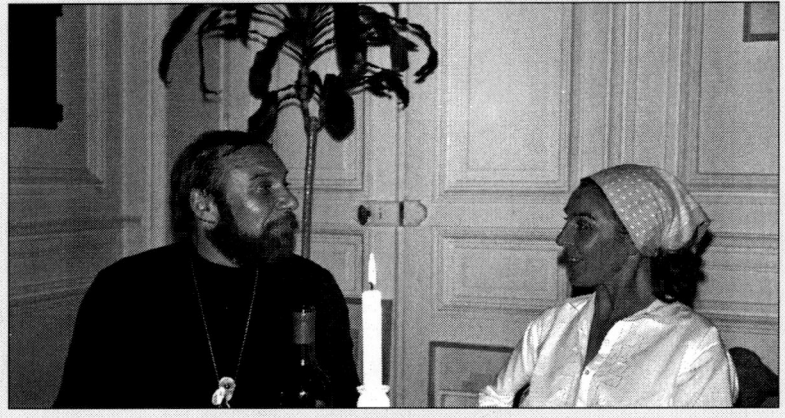

Top: O.R., Maria Schell & Werner Linssen, Bauhaus Museum, 1982
Bottom: O.R. & Emmy de Martelaere, Paris, 1978

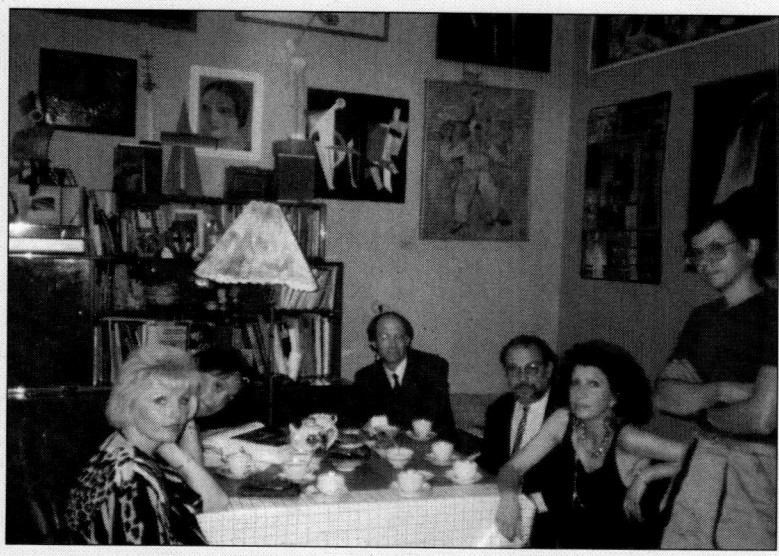

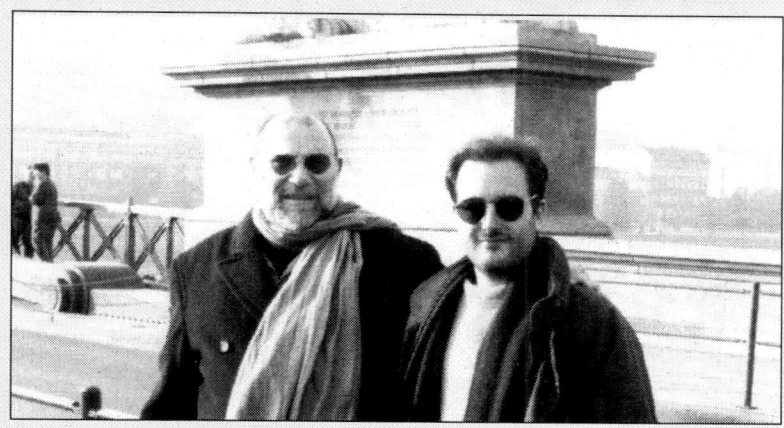

Top: At the Rodchenko house, Moscow, 1989
Bottom: O.R. & Iair Rosencrantz, Vienna, 1993

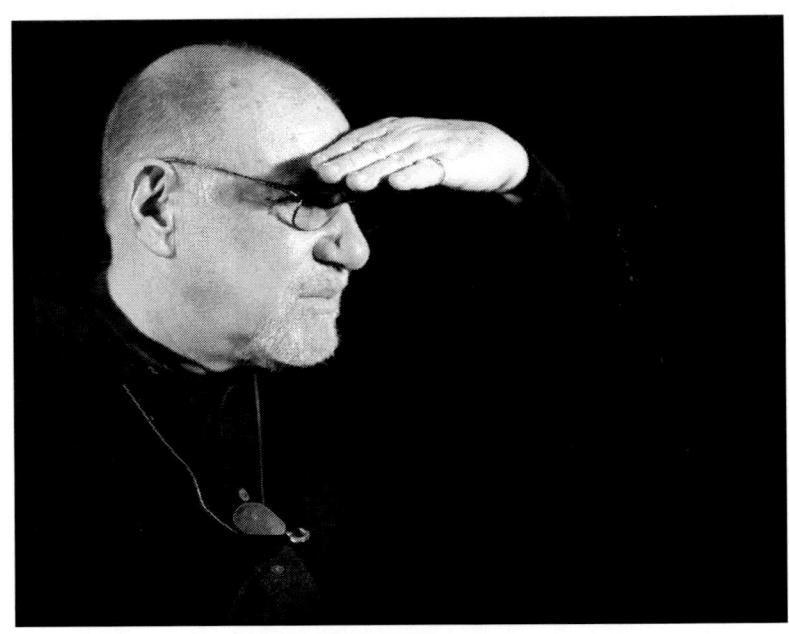

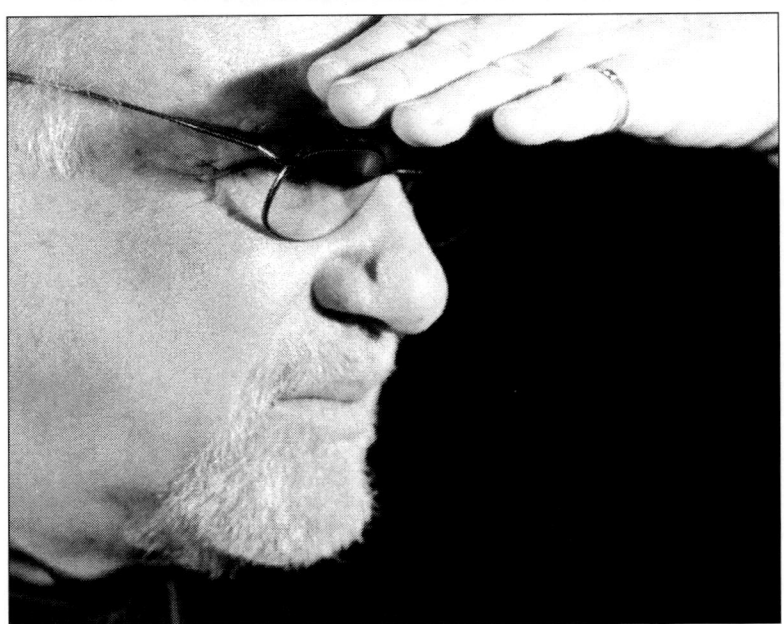

ABOUT BOOKS

*U*npacking my library, the walls came down. I had moved into my new lodgings in early April, and though the stagnant coldness of bare branches now re-placed the leaves of autumn, still my bookshelves lay fallow. It was as if this lifetime of collection refused the compression into a given order: how would I organize them?

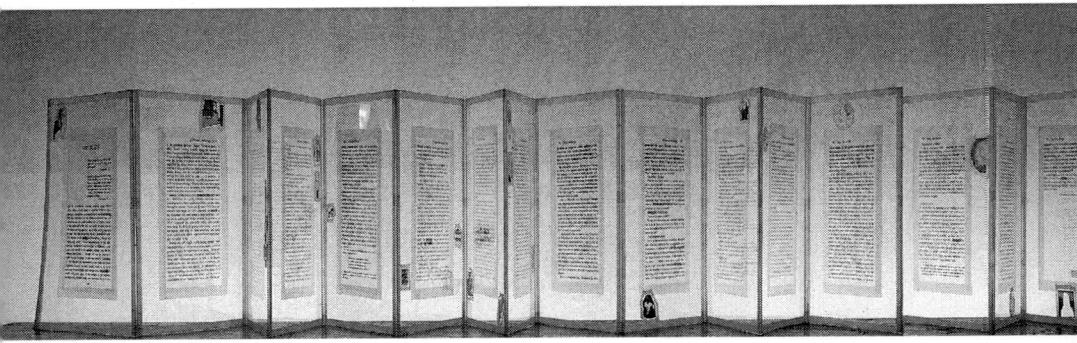

metaphors of a magnifico
JEAN-MICHEL RABATÉ

The last decades of the twentieth century have witnessed the breakdown of an older semiotic paradigm that took for granted a stark and obvious opposition between the domains of the analogical and of the digital. Thus for Barthes in the sixties, the productions of the visual world could not be readily equated with a "language." The status of language cannot be granted to communication by analogy, since the idea of language presupposes a man-made code of differential units such as words. For instance, if one wants to describe a press photograph as a "message," one has to first own that this message is produced by the uneasy coincidence of two codes, the analogical and the digital. The analogical offers reproductions of reality that imitate its feeling of a visual continuity and homology; this is what one experiences with drawings, paintings, films, and theatrical

As a way of generalizing, I would say that there is art, there is art history, and then there is the illustration of art history. Most of what we see when we say "this is a good painter" is simply an illustration of art history. Art is more difficult to recognize.

By alphabetical order, by date, by provenance, by my own biography? No order com-pelled me to the open boxes and closed typography of past flirtations. Of course, not all of them were mine. Many a borrowed and stolen text were hidden between

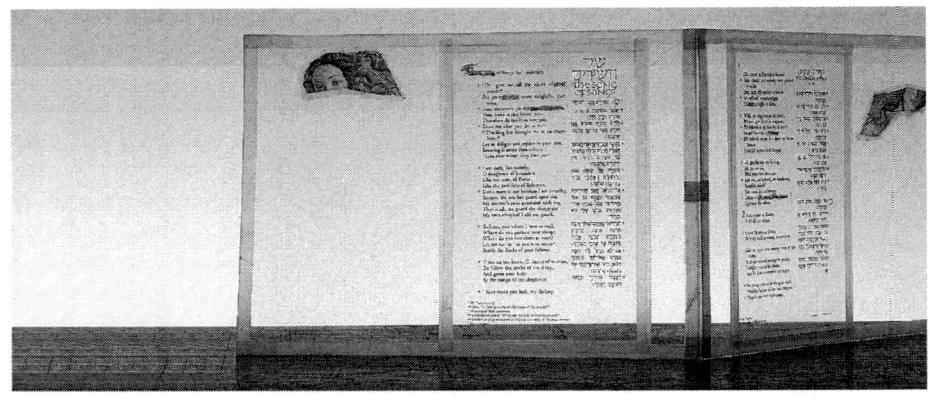

performances. These stage an analogon to reality, and borrow from reality its seamless appearance, while framing devices such as text, titles, captions, or articles (in the case of a newspaper showing photographs and text together) fulfill their function of commentary by relying on the digital or differential code we all understand if we share a given language. This is why Barthes can assert that a photograph is a "message without a code." The knowledge implied by any deciphering of a photograph is bounded by what our perception allows us to understand. Of course, Barthes can show readily that the dream of a purely referential image does not exist, and that any photograph relies on the juxtaposition of non-coded iconic message ("things" that can be recognized once photographed), coded-iconic messages (with all the layers of allusions and meanings one can "read" in effects of perspective, connotation, distortion, and so on) and finally linguistic messages (the caption and the commentaries that may or may not accompany the image).

Barthes famously reversed his point of view in which his later texts on photography, especially in his very last book, *Camera Lucida*, in which he claimed that he was returning to realism. At the

Very few people do art, and we cannot tell whether it is good or bad, because if it is art it opens new roads.

When I look at a work, and I don't know how to eat it: maybe this is art.

the arcs and peaks of my ex libris. Of course, not all of them had been read, and nor would they be. There were, however, three precious volumes to divine such oversights: in the wake of these books of books, other text was ornament. One night in

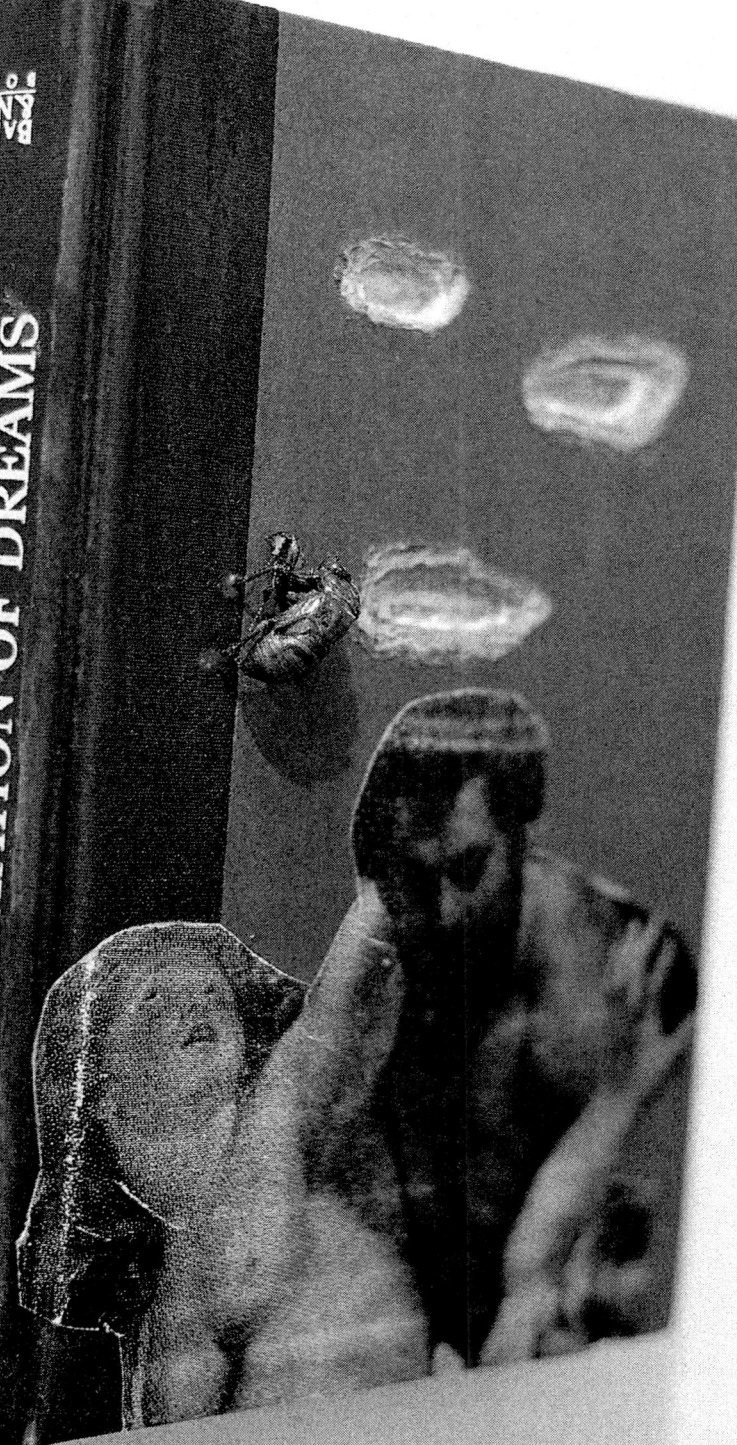

late May, I sensed that time had stopped, as if to probe the limits of my desires to put these books in their final place. Throughout the staircases and corridors of my new home, the sound of Monsieur de Sainte-Colombe's students metered my search

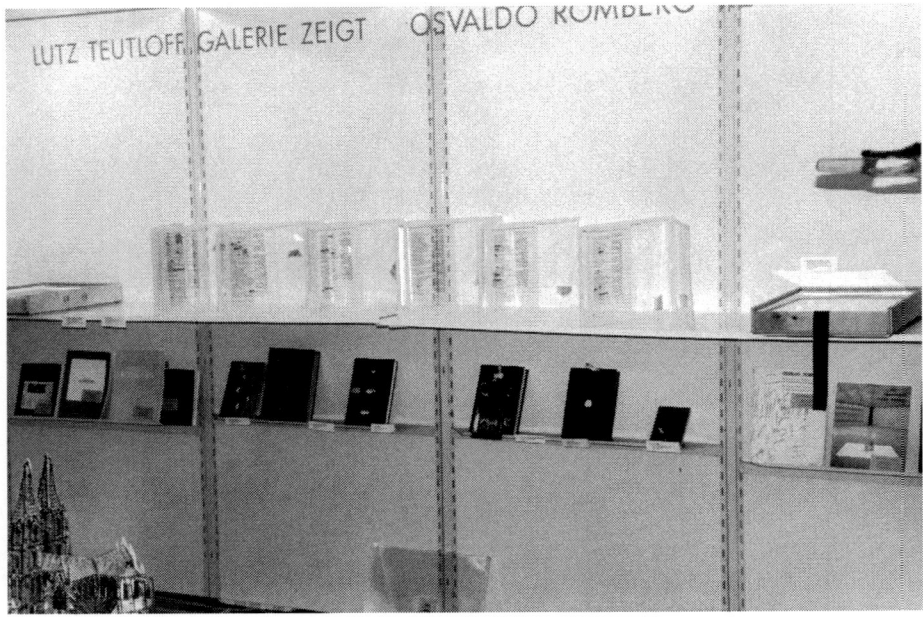

same time, the emergence of the new technology of digitalization changed the paradigm: it was possible to digitalize everything, from sound to images. Any spectral continuum of pitches, harmonies, intensities, dispatched along electrical circuits that would then re-compose them on other supports and would be perceived elsewhere by the viewer or listener. This shift is relevant to understand the evolution of Osvaldo Romberg's work. He began his career as a strict Barthesian, displaying next to reproductions of famous paintings their entire visual code that underpins our perception of their shapes and colors. By doing this, he showed that the analogical was always contaminated by the digital, that the very matter of the represented material could be read according to codes that structure our perception. However, he did not turn his back on semiotics later as Barthes did in the course of time. He did not have to recant his scientific explorations. He engaged with more ambitious projects all hinging around the function of representation. His work can be inscribed under the broad banner of "Conceptual Art" – or better said, of any art that does not want to limit itself to the "retinal" variety. Yet it cannot be called just "non-retinal" as Duchamp seemed at the time

I am attracted to things I don't understand. They arrest me, and I try to look at what is happening. If I go by taste, I will only stop at things that I like immediately – this is bad. If I see something and I do not know what to make of it, I try to see it through. Sometimes you discover interesting things this way. I prefer art that doesn't look like art. If you go by taste, you really become redundant.

for the library's ideal space. A turn in the North Wing revealed a descending set of stairs that brought me to a heavy cellar door. How many vintages had been stocked here? How much dust had settled on how many years of testing, failure, rectification

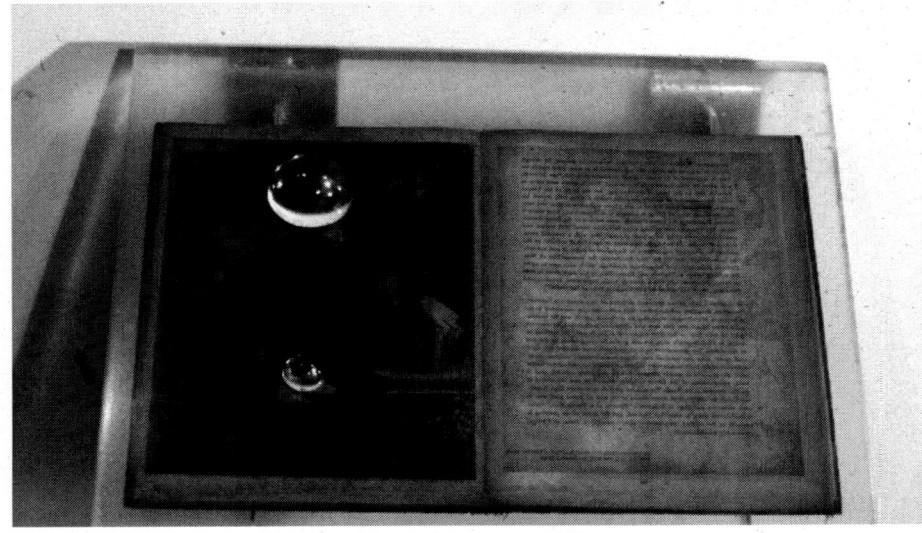

to suggest. His art is obsessed with the issue of reading. For Romberg, there is no picture that is not a text, no work that is not, in some way, a piece of writing. He gives new life to Derrida's dictum that "there is no 'outside-the-text' (*il n'y a pas de hors texte*)."

Such a textual condition of art in its "post-medium stage" is often symbolized by a book – a book that we cannot open or read, but that mutely begs for an impossible reading. Romberg's works can be called "descriptions" in the sense given to it by two important American writers, Gertrude Stein and Wallace Stevens. Wendy Steiner has analyzed how Stein's "portraits" are totally abstract and yet contain the essence of Picasso, Apollinaire, or Matisse.

But her reliance on verbal abstraction – that is, a refusal to "represent" anything by the means of words – was too extreme an analogon of abstract or non-representational painting. Osvaldo Romberg is closer to Wallace Stevens. First, like Stevens, he wants to make us think about what we see.

His central interrogation becomes: how can an image make us think? Is it shared by all in a non-problematic way? Do we

I cannot teach desire. It is in the body of a person. I have to distinguish between teaching and coaching. You don't teach people to run, you coach them, and sometimes you look at the position of the body, and consider the best techniques for the runner.

and refinement? Would there be anything left for me to exhume? The night ended, and yet my skin reflected no morning light. It took years to find my way back to the books in that darkness — there were no original coordinates from which to draw a

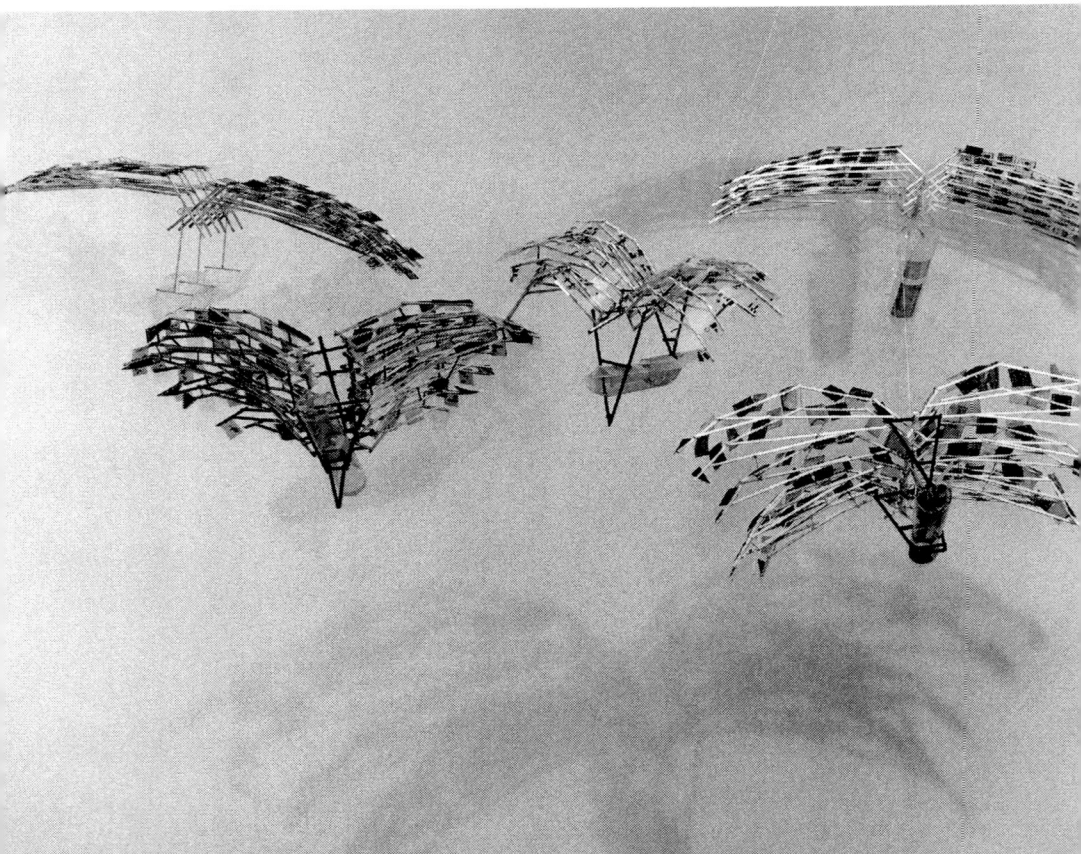

all see the same thing when we see an image that is not accompanied by its caption? How can painting make us think? Wallace Stevens has a poem entitled "Metaphors of a Magnifico" in which he asks us to make a thought experiment that has some bearing on what Osvaldo Romberg does with his viewers: he begins by sounding his theme, the vision of twenty men crossing a bridge to go into a village, and he asks whether each man walking on this bridge will have a different perception or whether they will all see the same thing. Hence: "Twenty men crossing a bridge,/ Into a village,/ Are twenty men crossing twenty bridges/ Into twenty villages/ Or one man crossing a single bridge into a village."

Of course, the poem continues, this divide between unanism and solipsism is old hat, it is an "old song", and it is safer to return to pure tautology: "Twenty men crossing a bridge,/ into a Village/ Are/ Twenty men crossing a bridge, / Into a Village." Yet this iteration is not satisfactory: the mind of the poet wanders, and he remains hesitant facing an all too "certain" meaning:

> "The boots of the men clump
> On the boards of the bridge.
> The first white walls of the village

> Rise through fruit-trees.
> Of what was it I was thinking?
> So the meaning escapes.
>
> The first white wall of the village...
> The fruit-trees..."

It is, of course, not a description of a "real" landscape – but we might as well be taken in; or imagine one. If we pose this naïve question, we'll have to follow the poet on his dubitative course. But where are the "metaphors" And who is this "Magnifico"? Let's assume that the "Magnifico" is what remains of the Romantic ideal of the Artist who battles heroically with paradoxes and incompatible codes. We will then realize that the concept of "metaphor" is to be taken literally – In Greek, that is, as "transportation" or "moving". If we have read the poem to the end, we have already crossed the bridge, whether it be literal or figural. We have accomplished the "metaphor" ourselves and we are therefore the poet's metaphors. Which is why the title has to be in the plural: "we" (whoever that may be) are more than one.

This is exactly what happens with Osvaldo Romberg's visual works. It is to such bridges between texts and images that

path. The headache of my still encased library would wake me the next day and the days after that. No matter how hard I tried, I would never find again that sliver of hope, the flight of stairs and its interminable morning. I never saw the catacombs again. Clearly, another tack was in order. In an act of desperation, I threw one box

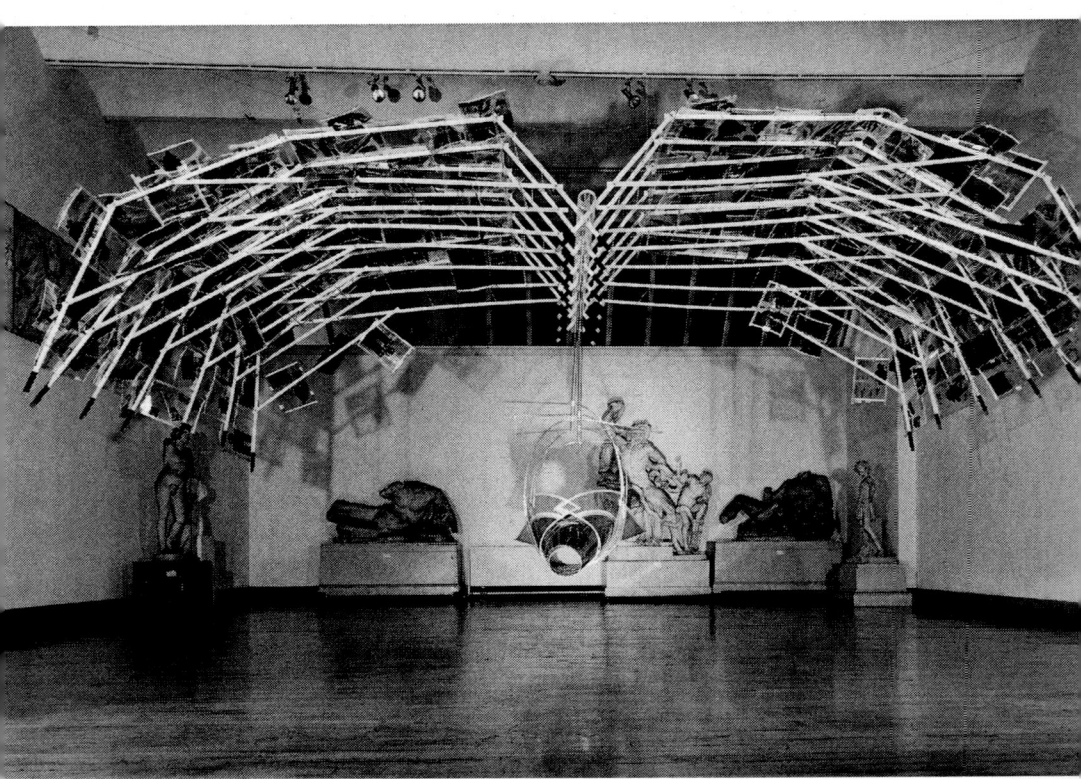

they carry us. They are both "descriptions" and the theory of descriptions; they are visual analogs that are also "texts" in themselves. Their reticent textuality and their metaphorical literalness force us to make (and remake continuously) our world. If they describe, it is as Stevens said, that is, "without a place" – another term for what can be construed as perpetual exile. Let us hear the poet once more since his words seem to apply to Romberg's project with all their force of conviction:

"Description is revelation. It is not
The thing described, nor facsimile.

It is an artificial thing that exists,
In its own seeming, plainly visible,

Yet not too closely the double of our lives,
Intenser than any actual life could be,

A text we should be born that we might read,
More explicit than the experience of sun

And moon... (...)

Thus the theory of description matters most
It is the theory of the word for those

For whom the word is the making of the world,
The buzzing world and lisping firmament.

It is a world of words to the end of it,
In which nothing solid is its solid self."

from the highest landing I could find. It did not trace a gainly arc; it simply frittered on its way down. My gardener picked up the pieces, and I hear talk that his son has put them to some use. Unable to make my mind, I made gifts of my library,

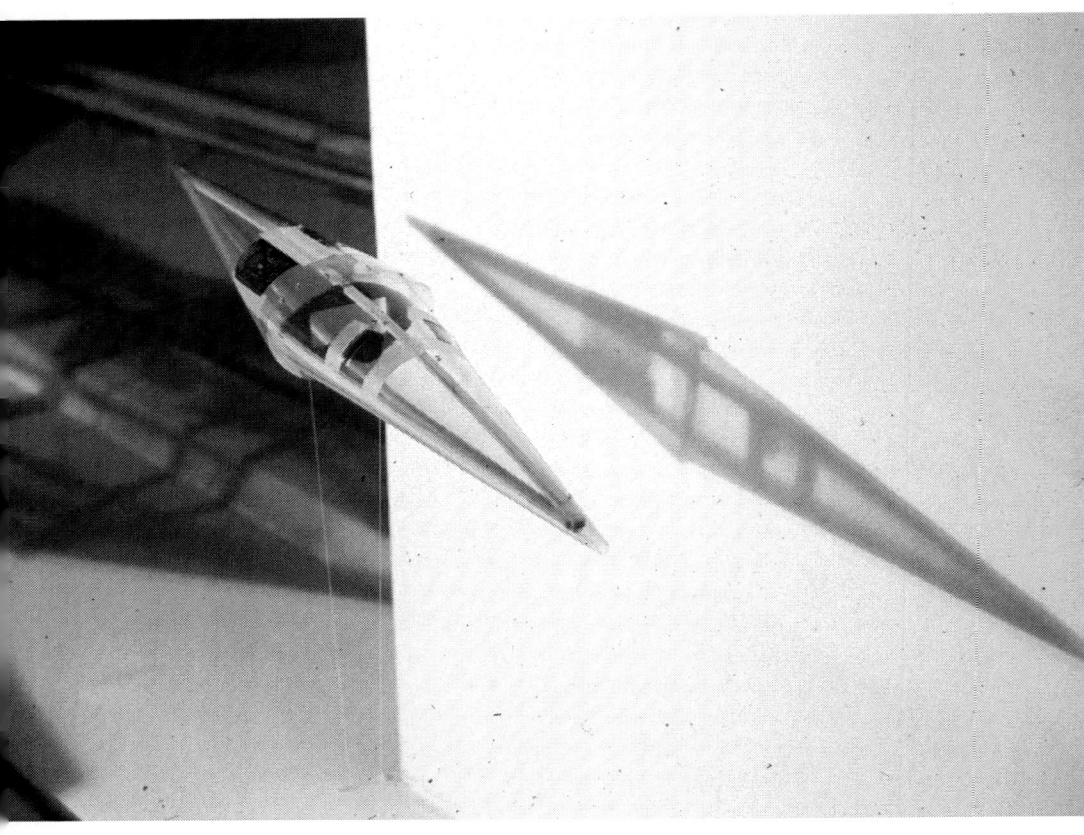

from book to book work
DIANA FRANSSEN

Osvaldo Romberg has made the book medium his own, yet at the same time tampers with its definition. However, a book remains a book even if the artist ignores its essential qualities. A book can't be estranged from its meaningful, linguistic history. What is more, the question of what a book is, is revived again when an artist appropriates it as a medium. The artists' book takes up a position at that junction where art, documentation, and literature converge.

Romberg's books are typically versatile and have a richness of expression. This isn't only evident from the exceptional, material quality of the publications, but also from the experimental nature of his projects, the scientific research that takes place through the artist's eyes and the contextual irony – without cynicism but with a vicious undertone.

I do not teach drawing. You cannot teach drawing as a native concept, you teach drawing in the style of Degas or Rembrandt or Ingres or Matisse. There is not good or bad drawing, merely schools of drawing, schools of painting, etc.

thereby displacing some of the burden. The cooks made a broth from Fourier's descriptions of Egypt; some believed it tasted of saffron. In the winter, some stuffed their rafters with outdated dictionaries while others fed the furnace with inscrutable foreign monographs. At first I was quite curious about all the uses towards which

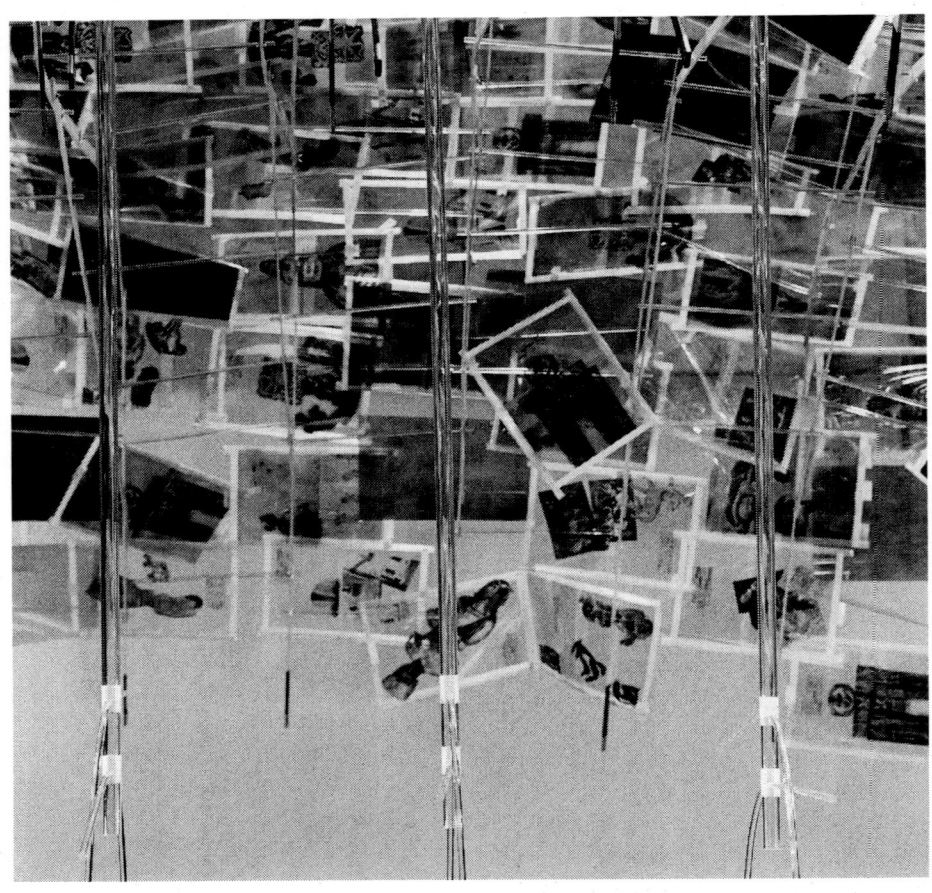

Romberg's books from the nineteen sixties, like his collaborations with the poets Elizabeth Azcona Cranwell and Alejandra Pizarnik, are similar to so-called Livres de Peintres – publications in which an artist and writer reinforce each other's strengths. Here the poet's language acts as an object with which the artist engages in a visual relationship. This gives rise to the actual art in the immediate time and space of the observer and reader.

Later on we see books being created that act as conceptual spaces, like for instance in *Dilemma between Faith and Knowledge* (1996), or as an instrument for social change in *Civilization* (2001). Sometimes the book acts as an accusation, the outside of which is already enough to sense what's on the inside, or even to fear this. In other instances an attempt is made to destroy the book's function as an intimate reading source by shutting it tight forever, by presenting it as a multiple, or by exhibiting it as a rare auratic object on a specially made shelf.

As well as having a poetic, art historical and literary component, Romberg's book works also have a highly social and political context. Clement Greenberg's formalist doctrine turned art into a socially irrelevant phenomenon with the result that the gap between Culture with a capital C and the modern world widened. This cultural philosophy acts as a provocation to Romberg and forms one of the major aspects in his work with which he explains his views. In fact by using the book as a medium, the democratic mass medium par excellence, to question and to use it as a work of art in a small edition, or even as a one-off, the gap between art and life is subjected to fundamental study.

In his books, which are an indivisible part of his body of work, he gives expression to a culturally critical viewpoint. Romberg's visual language is highly symbolic and permeated with references to history, Christendom and the myth of the artist. In his work contradictions like holy and profane, death and rebirth, history and actuality, nature and civilisation, 'high' and 'low' culture, old and new or creativity and destruction are always present. For him the book functions as a critical tool for ideological and political analyses. He explores historical and contemporary reality and comes up with results that dethrone so-called value-free art production and challenge the seemingly social and political neutrality of the exhibition space.

my books had been redirected. Yet everything everywhere pointed to failed systems and falling signifiers. I recall one particular afternoon of fury in which I strew three boxes of French romantics across my studio's floor. Next winter, I resolved to send for outside help.

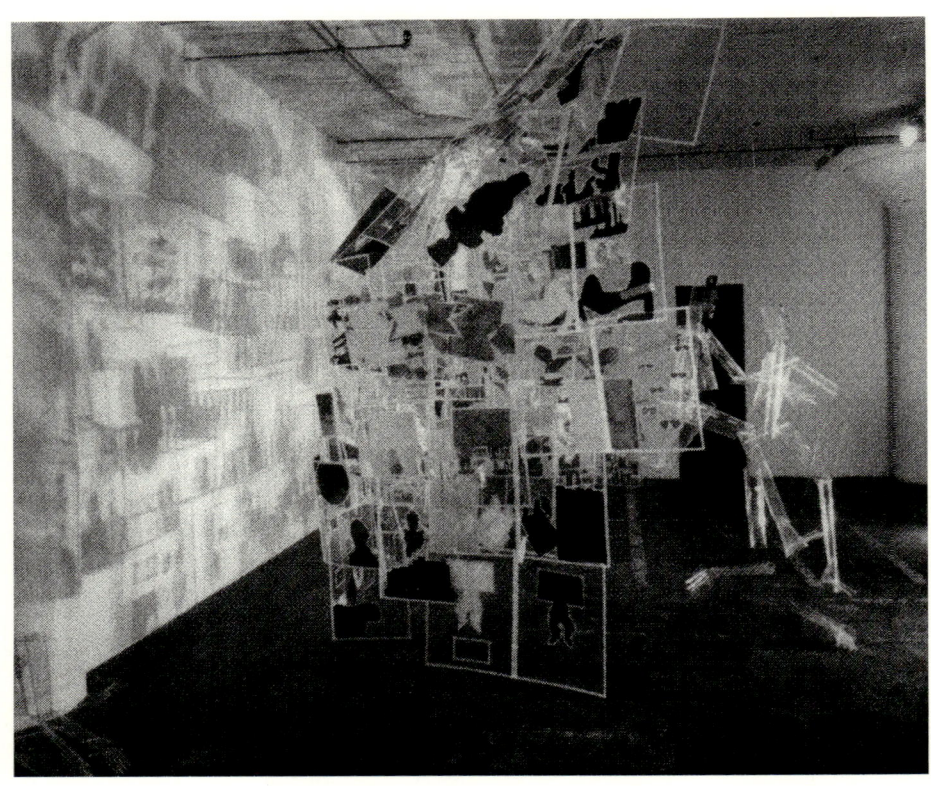

*I don't dream. In real life I only dream
when a disaster is imminent. I dream how
to get out of the disaster, but very rarely
do I dream.*

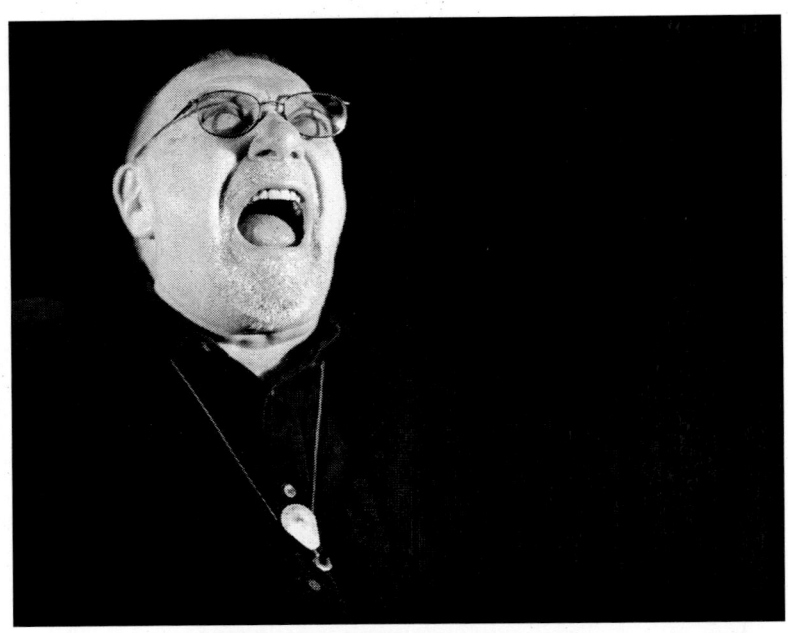

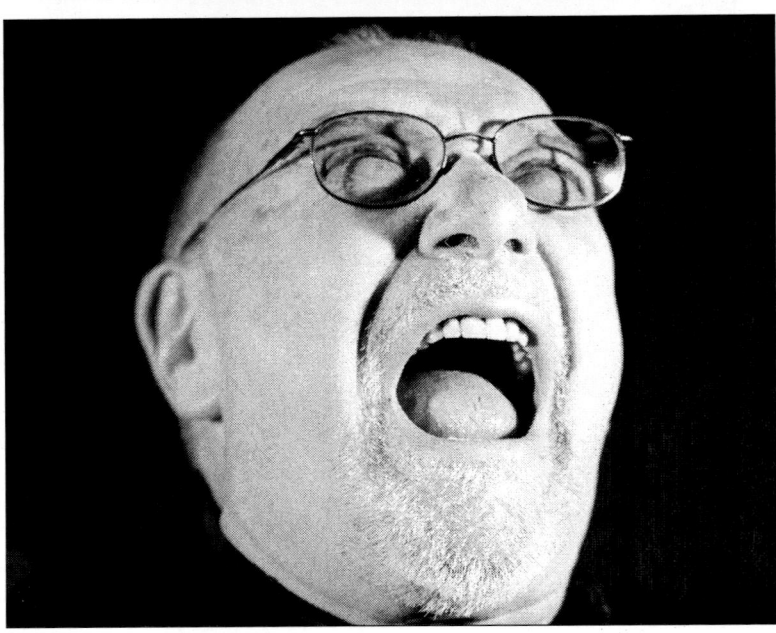

ABOUT
INSTALLATION

A *dubious joke that I keep telling: Two country preachers embark on a stroll to facilitate digestion. Approaching the edges of their hamlet a dilemma appears, quite literally, on the horizon; it is becoming dark out, will they continue outward or turn back toward their humble parish? They idle, indecisive, it becomes darker still,*

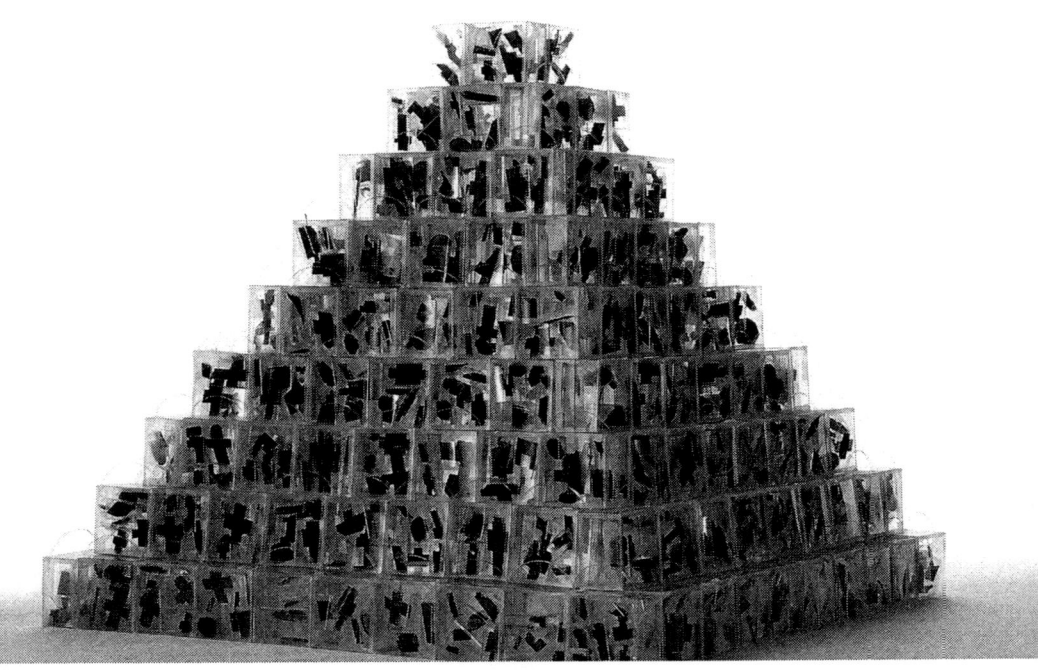

referentiality: the translocation of architecture towards narrativity. osvaldo romberg's architectural discourses

LORAND HEGYI

REFERENCE: ARCHITECTURE

Architecture, as a spatial organization with symbolic messages and socio-cultural representations, with historical connections and mythical, religious, and spiritual competencies, is the main reference in Osvaldo Romberg's multi-faceted and multi-disciplinary œuvre. By handling formalized, allegorically perceived, sometimes even venerated, fetishized, and absolutized contingents of form legitimized by cultural memory and often detached from their original architectural context, Osvaldo Romberg pursues a consistent dual strategy linked to a colorful cultural production. This strategy localizes his œuvre at various levels and in different areas.

I divide my work into three periods. The first is that from Argentina, the second began after I left Argentina. There is a third period that I showed only once or twice, around the time my son was born in the early 80s, I did a series of paintings about surrealism. They were a big mistake, and I never show that work.

after a short time they can distinguish only silhouettes behind and in front of them. A third option becomes apparent, to confabulate a temporary shelter from the diverse materials — ornaments, prophylactics, prayer pamphlets, fetishes, almanacs,

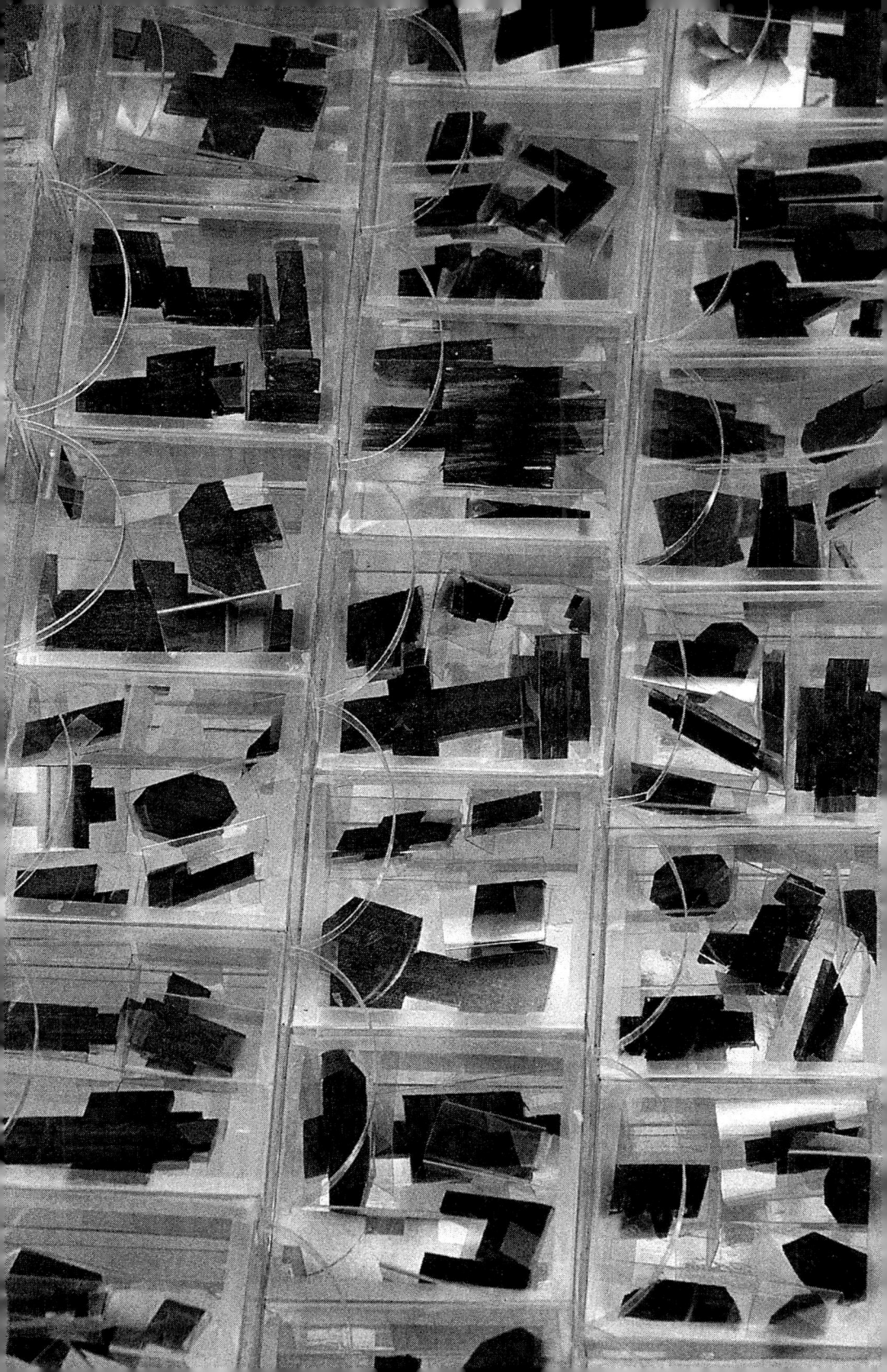

and astrological apparatuses. Slumbering shortly thereafter in their fabrication the clergymen are subject to unanticipated variations of meteorology and hallucination. They dream themselves awash in the brackish waters of the Aral sea – or have I got

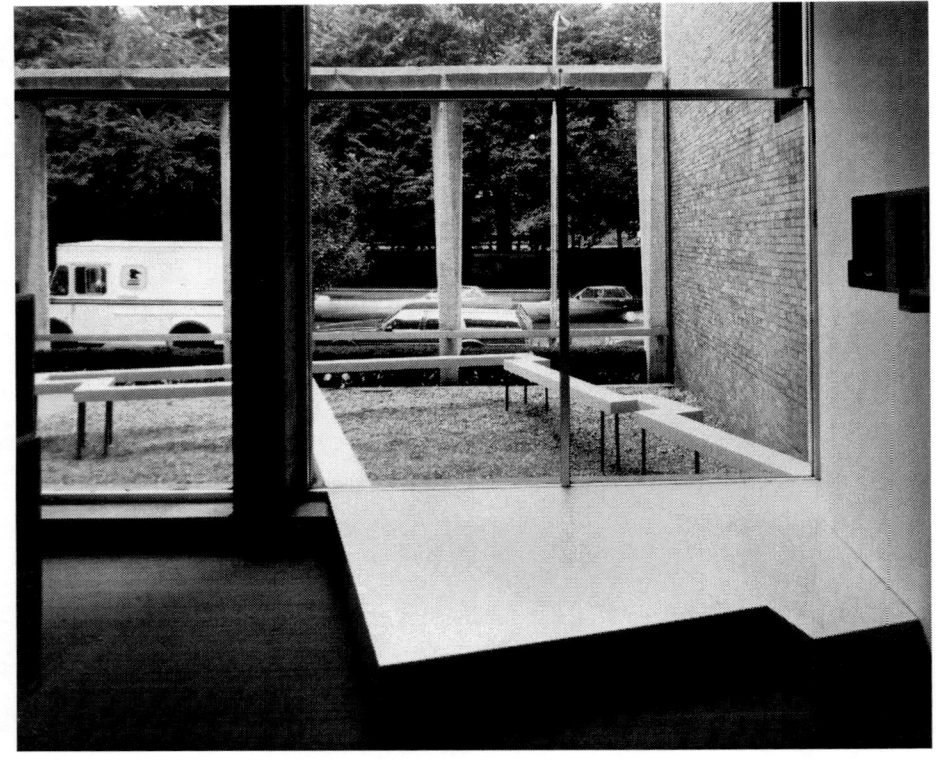

On the one hand, he works with the analytical deconstruction of linguistic elements and the décor of architectural design of different historical eras, cultures, and religions. He focuses on the symbolic use of architecture as a representative system of values, as a collective and conventional model of thought. Romberg creates new potential contexts, novel modes of interpretation, and surprising connections, intentionally and probingly confronting cultural and historical realities with linguistic rules and forms of communication. This bold deconstruction is performed with rational precision and laboratory-like discipline, and the new settings he creates allow for innovative and open thoughts.

NARRATIVITY

On the other hand, Osvaldo Romberg also moves towards a new, picturesque, and universal narrativity. His tales about myths and paradigms, allegories and metaphors, ancient historical experiences and recurrent utopias search for their own authentic addressee. This narrativity uses architecture as a vocabulary to describe certain events and the manner in which they unfold. This new narrativity

The first period, the Argentinian period, was probably most influenced by Group Cobra. I was more popular as a print maker in then, in the very early 60s – I won the National Award in print making, at the salon of Cordoba, and showed with two important artists of Argentinian figuration at that time, Planas and Cornet.

it backwards again, the reflections stop you, was each-other the perceived? When they wake once more a dampness is just perceptible in the red clay. They turn back. /// Have you attended the boat races? I have never seen such magnificent acci-

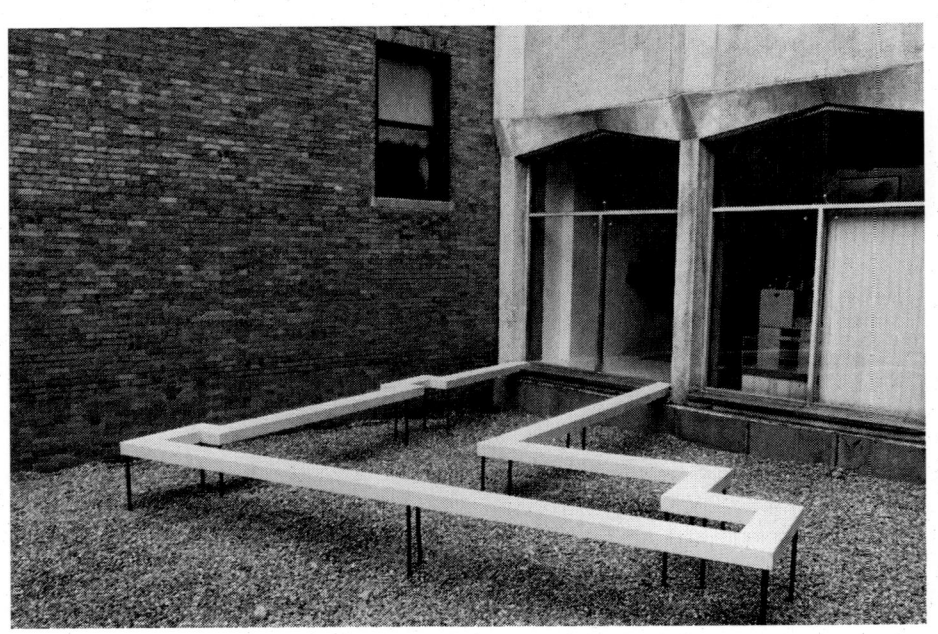

incorporates architectural forms as examples, as sensually perceived material images capable of objectifying archetypical conflicts and struggles, antagonisms, and symbioses. It is precisely at this level that Osvaldo Romberg's argumentation acquires an almost gigantic dimension, at least as far as the broad range or referentiality – and thus topicality and applicability – is concerned. Aaron Levy comments on this phenomenon as follows: "…Romberg deals with architectural plans as if they belong to the domain of natural history rather than architecture proper. The Erechtheion temple attacks the Barcelona pavilion; in this scenario, architecture becomes infected with bacteria and disintegrates as a representation of contemporary political phenomena in the areas of ecology, war, cloning, and mutation."

DUAL STRATEGY

Behind this dual strategy pursued by Romberg we find a fresh historical vision which can be comprehended in the context of global referentiality. As Hagai Segev puts it: "Osvaldo Romberg's art embodies an all-encompassing, all-embracing cultural vision, crossing territorial borders as well as the borders of culture and period. Romberg's historical

I came to America for the first time in 1963 to do shows in Washington and Miami. The things that I saw blew my mind: pop art, multiples, etc. When I came back to Argentina, I began to do strange things and the Argentinean press said it was over for me.

I did multiples, I did prints on plexiglass which I warmed and bended to make three-dimensional forms. I began to synthesize the figure almost to the point of abstraction.

dents. *Thirty or forty behemoths jockeying before the glaring sun; one vessel is bound to lose its orientation, to turn abruptly amidst the confusion of a hundred competing commands and drive its prow into the walls of another, laying bare and doomed*

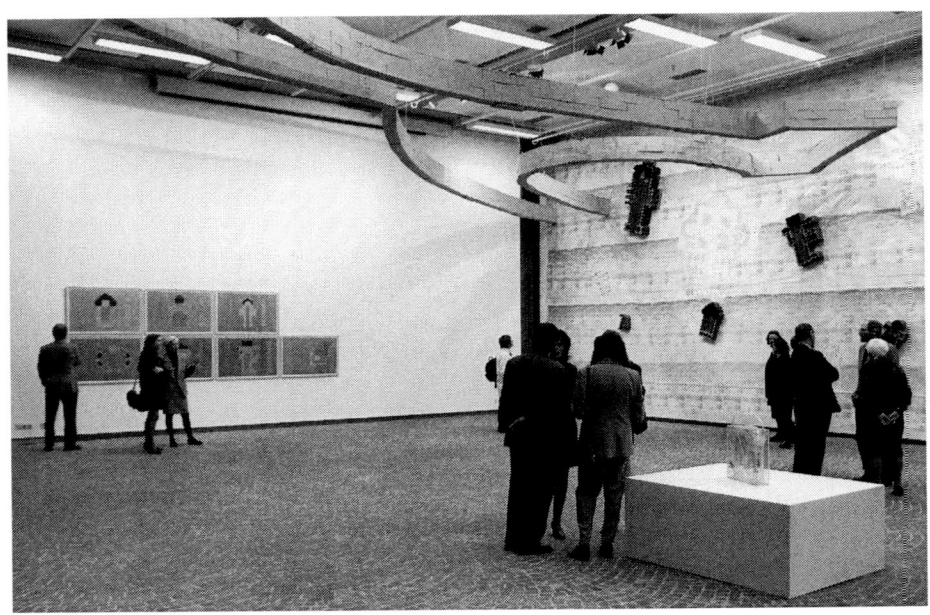

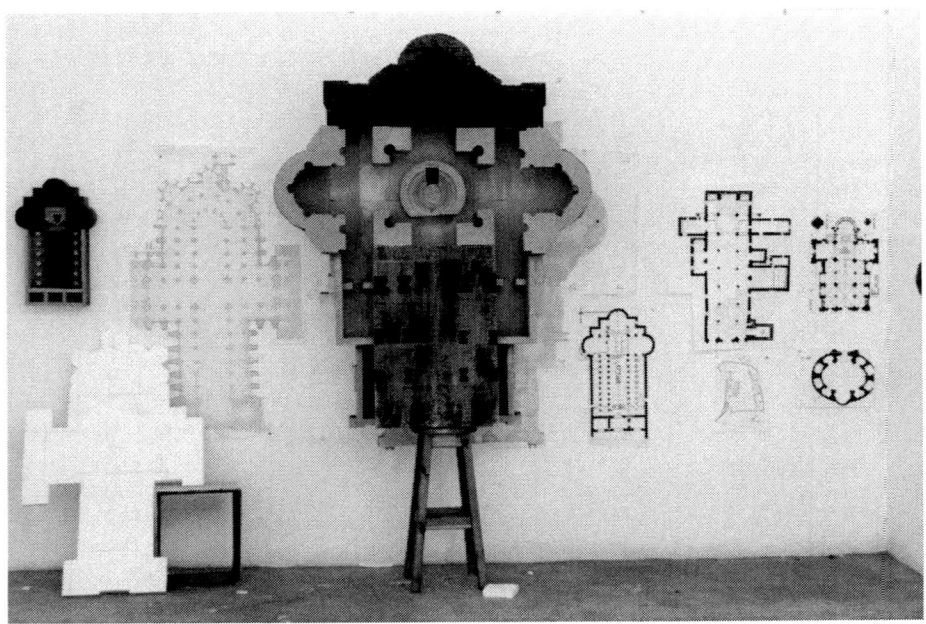

vision does not limit itself to one particular culture, but attempts to study human culture as one global whole." This global whole allows for a bold and provocative confrontation of various cultures and cults, epochs and formalized systems of values, cosmic visions, and mythological explanations of the world which result in an abstraction of human attitudes. Osvaldo Romberg includes references to the entire history of culture, he accompanies certain situations and questions on their way through different eras and cultures, and he tests their long-term validity and authenticity.

In order to be able to carry out this investigation in various contexts, representative systems need to be transferable and adaptable. This means, for example, that the wall of a building or the ground plan of a house needs to be rendered abstract and transferred to the quasi-pictorial level, serving as an "abstract picture," so that the linear system can function as a symbolic motif independent of architecture. Romberg uses this alienated form – acting as a universal metaphor – and confronts it with other logo-like forms taken from other contexts.

TRANSLOCATION

The permanent translocation of representative architectural contingents of form alludes to Romberg's key questions, i.e. those pertaining to the modes of presenting values which certain cultures and specific historical or ethical, linguistic or religious micro-communities, need to pursue their vital strategies. The architectural design of spaces, with its symbolic, metaphorical, ideological, and sociological connotations, results in specific places where people can get together, or which they are able to have permission to enter, or from which they are excluded. This architectural design of spaces plays a pivotal role in our lives and our symbolic organizations such as power structures and politics, but also for the collective ideological and mythological principles of each community. Osvaldo Romberg explores this capacity and the symbolic power associated with spatial design by directly comparing different systems and design concepts.

What happens with different contingents of form as they are transplanted into other cultural, historical, and mental contexts has to do with the artist's own micro-history, his life-long nomadic existence, and his never-ending translo-

the skeletons of both crafts. They splinter and explode, scatter their components onto the waves. A naïve science of their reconstruction is attaining popularity here amongst the underburdened gentry, who have committed great storehouses and en-

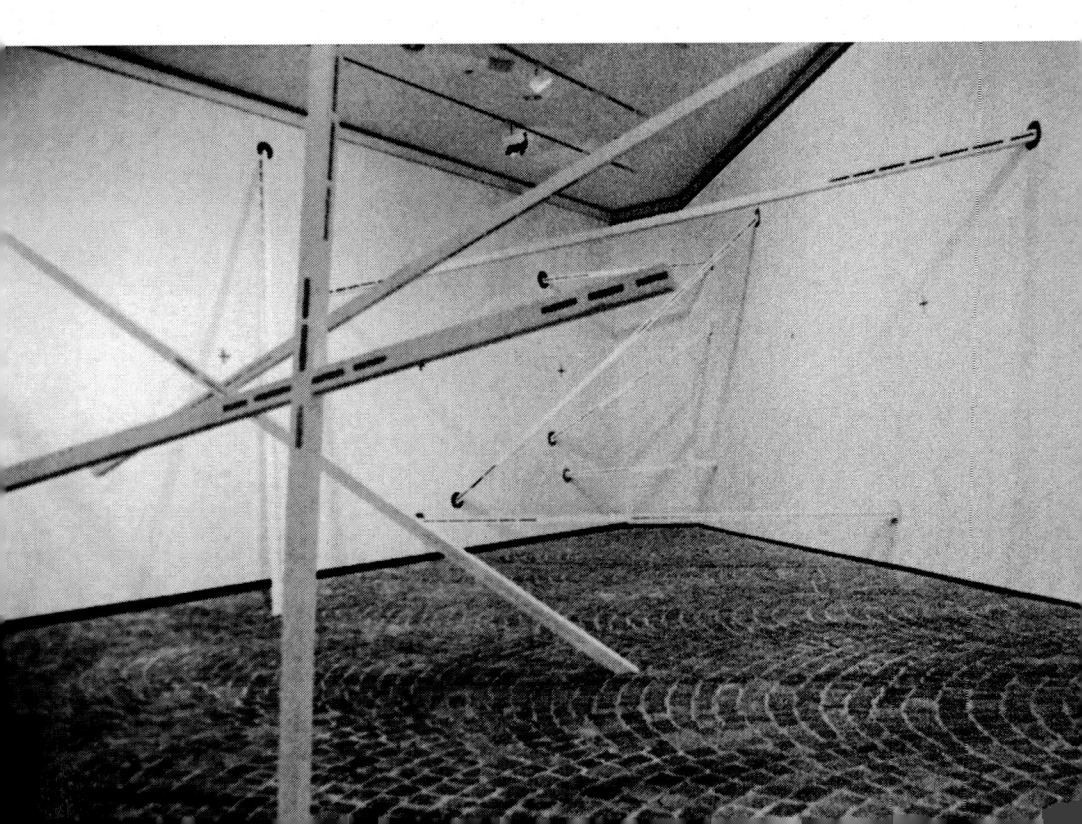

cation. Romberg's paraphrases are embedded in his personal experiences and micro-history, although in his work he mainly deals with universal metaphors. Osvaldo Romberg is one of those artists who radically reassesses historical referentiality and recontextualizes artistic strategies in complex historical, social, and cultural processes. He moves naturally in a historical context, with different historical, social, and cultural models serving as immediate references to his quasi-architectural installations and objects.

PERSONAL HISTORY

In this connection Iair Rosencranz rightly talks about a personal reading of history, one which visualizes historical events by metaphors translated into somebody's own situation, even though these metaphors always include universal concepts and dimensions. "The argument of locus in the work of Romberg is as irrelevant as the crisis of representation; he bypasses the arguments by dealing with his own rules to establish a base for metaphorical manipulation of history. Transcending the debate towards a new history of civilization, Romberg proposes a personal reading of it, or in Borgesian terms, he views the situation as "the history of a

From 1968 to 1969, I began making landscape-based sculptures, and then I passed directly to land art, but with a conceptual approach. "The Landscape as Idea" was the beginning of this in 1969 and then again in 1970.

ergies to the preservation of these failed voyages; the twin technologies of divination and geometry are mustered in the isolation of that moment of historical paroxysm. Yet there also exists a vocal and active contingent aghast at such misuse, who at-

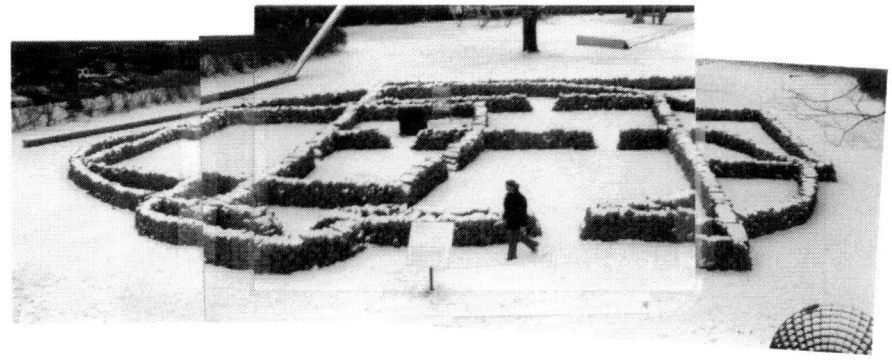

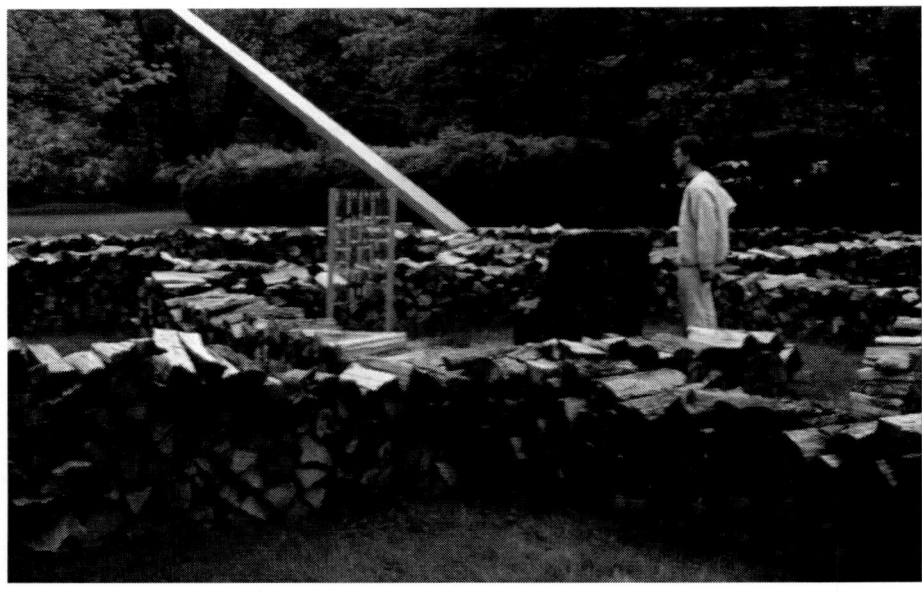

few metaphors." This approach enables the artist to play with history, art, architecture and science. The science proposed here is to be viewed as another metaphor, seen perhaps as an equivalent of Darwinian de-mystification of nature held in place against the pre-established romanticization of natural forces. As the artist he is the catalyst for new combinations, permutations and associations.

Osvaldo Romberg, as has already been pointed out, works in a global cultural, sociological, and historical context. Every formation and cultural design and every mythological, philosophical, religious, or scientific concept may have have universal, global, topical, and relevant messages. Viewed from this angle, time and space play no exclusive or limited role; rather, they enrich potential references. But Romberg also addresses the personal interpretation of cultural and historical events and specifies abstract micro-communities. Historical awareness finds its inherent arguments in real and specific events, rather than in abstract, external, and teleological explanations. As Romberg compares different cultural and historical events with each other, he remains within the context of real history, i.e. he raises real questions about the relevance or irrelevance of certain

mental and cultural systems. As a permanent revision and correction of earlier interpretations of cultural formations takes place in a real historical process, Romberg articulates possible questions and possible confrontations.

REFERENTIALITY

Thus Osvaldo Romberg's geometric formations both relate to historical, architectural, and philosophical contexts and, at the same time, to art – immanent and formerly phenomenological instances. These geometric formations function as conveyers of a transference, in which references and connotations are transferred and rejected onto other formations without losing any of their ambivalence of form as cultural signs and as "purely formal phenomena." He testifies to the stormy era of utopian, avant-garde architecture, when it tried to design sites for the future ideal society that sprang from a utopia of a world revolution.

In the same way he works with the ground plans of sacred Greek, Mesopotamian, Egyptian, or Jewish architecture, in which the room is seen as a spiritual site, a place for the presence of God, that is, as an "out of the-ordinary", of-

tempt to build homes and fuel furnaces from the wreckage. Indeed, not a few sturdy constructions have been enforced with the reclaimed pulp. And yet to the dismay of their inhabitants, the redirected materials cannot shed their aura. Peripatetic follow-

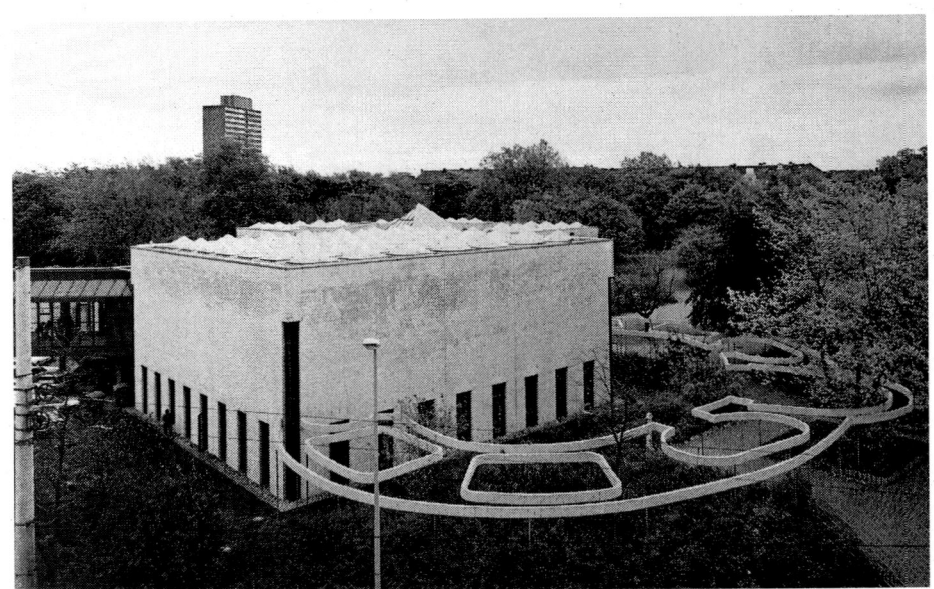

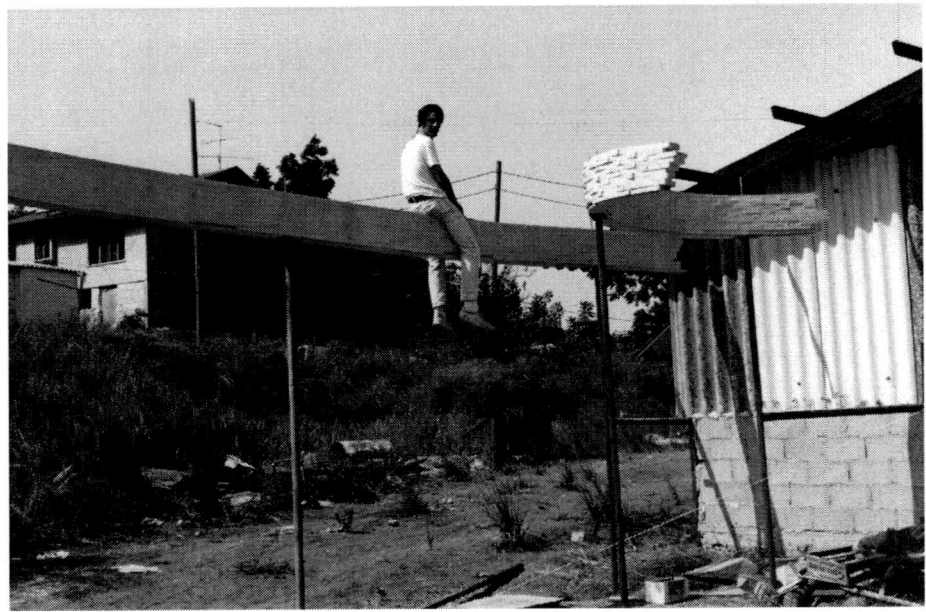

ten irrational place. The utopia of the avant-garde and the religious ideology of archaic epochs converted the architectural design into a presentation of moral values. When an artist of the 1980s and 1990s works with architectural and archæological models, we can conclude that the search for legitimate formal solutions no longer leads the artist in the direction of visions of the future, i.e., no longer to utopia, but to the past, which enables him to find thematically significant reserves of meaning.

Osvaldo Romberg creates mural objects and installations from the elements of different architectural structures, through which he creates intellectual and formal associations via the visual, sculptural conversation of the original formations, associations that break through the restricted time frame and produce new mental contexts between different ways of thinking, or between different value systems. By means of a consistent use of materials and color, Osvaldo Romberg nudges the viewer toward an interpretation of three-dimensional structures – originally based on more or less historically known architectural ground plans – as simultaneously being geometric, abstract from systems and complex models for an eventual spatial evolve-

Art is a train going fast, and if you are on the train, it is okay, but if you want to catch it then you need to run very fast.

ers of the races have begun to visit the structures, in ceaseless perambulant devotion to the erotics of so much recycled potency. /// I am sorry, I have been reading the dailies again, those garish, smeared pages still declaim our arrival at last, awash in

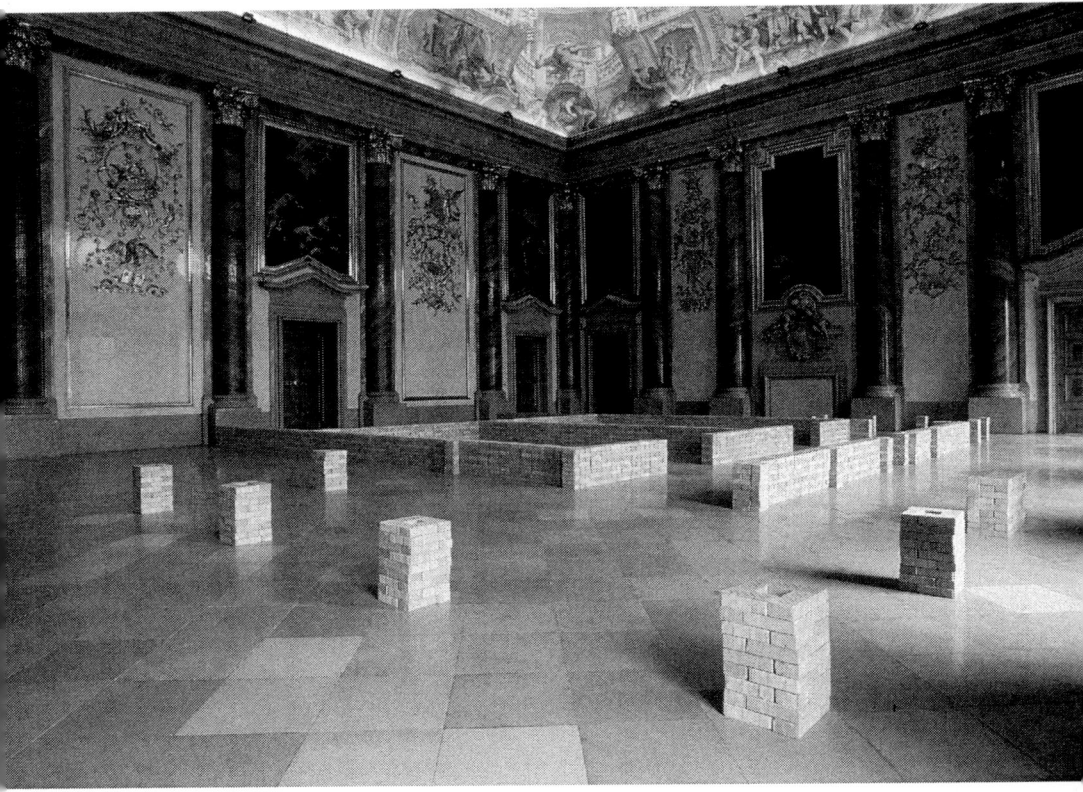

ment. On the one hand, this instigates a process of imaginary reconstruction of a former edifice in a diminutive form that is liberated from the original function of architecture for interpretation. On the other hand, this object can be seen as the starting point of a fictitious and imaginary self-generating practice, whereby the object incorporates the special suggestions and propositions of a subjective fictional language of signs, a language based on signals that originate in our cultural history. In this way, purely geometrical forms are not only interpretable as abstract shapes, but as cultural fragments. Romberg has tried to develop a very complex and open language of signs that can be understood as a practical and usable language in a visual, sculptural locality and also as a network of associations and indications for different ideas of utopia. In the fruitful tension between the directly confrontational – yet, on a formal level, surprisingly harmonious – fragments, he attempts to visualize the latent utopia that is not localized in the future but in the subjective observance of the past as a utopia that is poetically free and completely autonomous. The individual motifs, the parts or the entire ground plan of buildings (very often sacred architecture) function as the depository of latent messages that convey not always fully evident, clear-cut statements on time and the transitory, on transcendence and the mystery of loss. They are the source of quasi-archæological research that does not take the direction of objective, scientific reconstruction, but that of metaphorical, poetic, anthropological self-discovery in a cultural and mythological sense. Like the temples and cultic edifices on the city map of ancient Rome reconstructed by Osvaldo Romberg, the artist's objects stand like stations on the path he has taken in his search for his own cultural and anthropological focal point.

INTIMACY AND PUBLIC COMPETENCIES

Romberg reconstructs his intellectual, artistic, and personal path through epoch and art styles, through myths and philosophies, through continents and religions, to a metaphor of the eternally searching artist, who views his homeland not as something historically given, but as an environment that is intellectually, artistically, and ideologically created. An artist is for him an eternal wanderer, who consistently pursues his path through cultures and epochs so as to seek out his identity, his spiritual home,

168 | *a newness will not become worn — but do they also name a certain grim and leaden finality? I am unconvinced all the same; the dust must settle somewhere. I am aged enough now to see the nomad waiting at the edges — such darknesses surround us,*

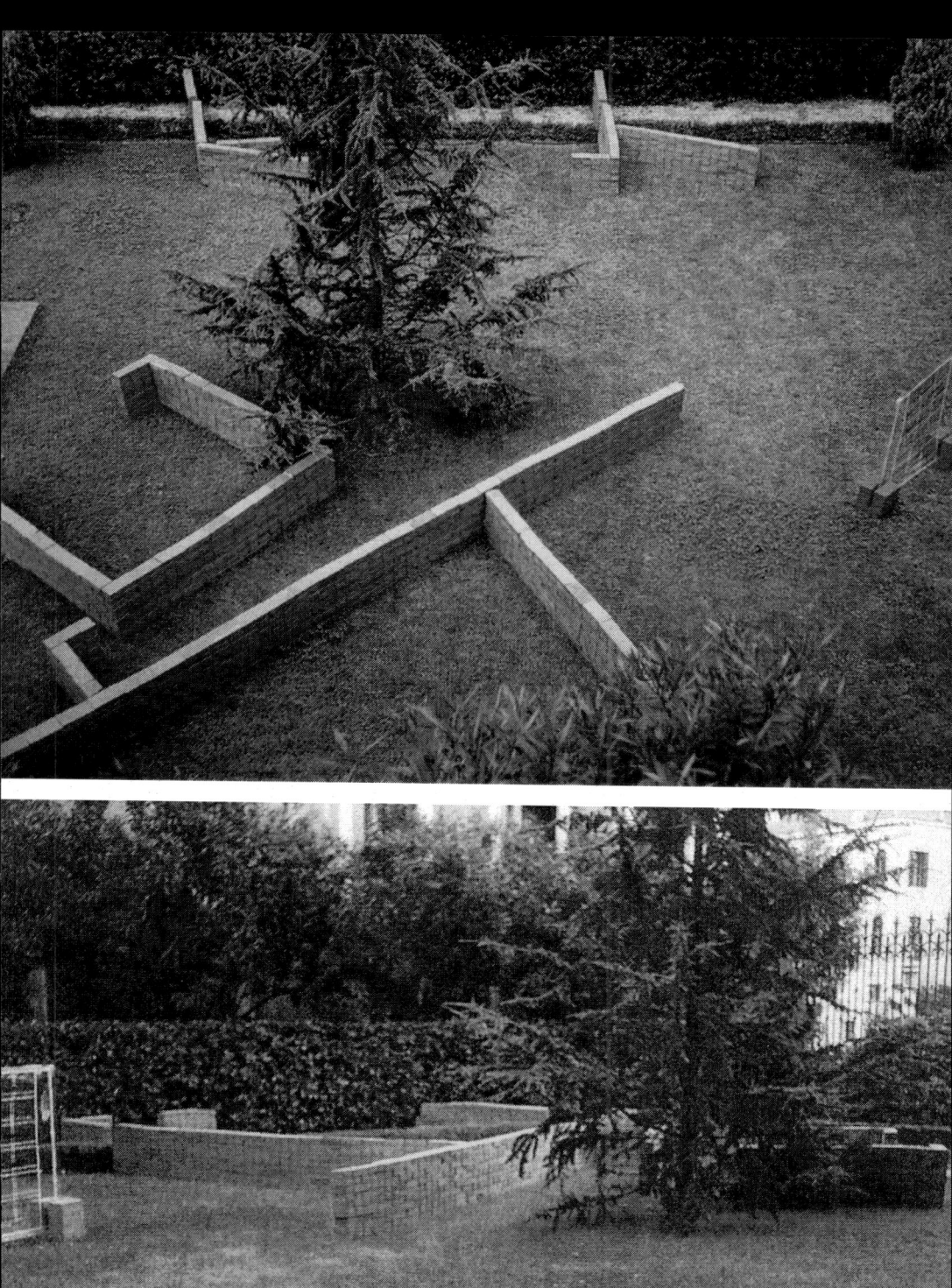

what could we do against them? — we will yet find ourselves cast out, supplanted,

relocated, dispersed, and quoted. I take my walks along the beach, and I can see

their masts on the horizon. Ibn Khaldun witnessed them astride horses as well, ap-

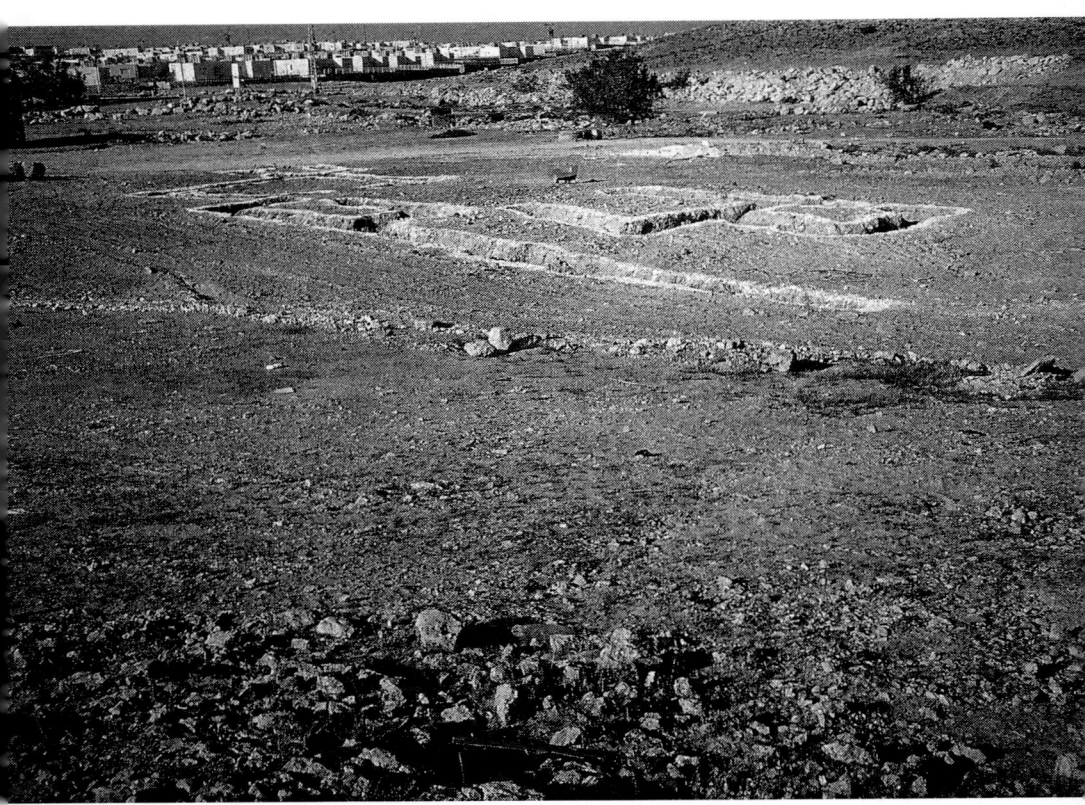

while he constructs his own utopia of an individually coherent mental world out of the raw material from the most diverse sources.

Thus it can be claimed that Osvaldo Romberg's position is typical and paradigmatic for the present sitation in the late 20th and early 21st centuries. His œuvre links, on the one had, utopian thinking of the classical avant-garde with the critical discourse on utopia in the epoch of postmodernism. He sees utopia as a historical phenomenon, determined by the different objective relationships and ideological, religious, and philosophical values. He relativizes utopia insofar as he confronts it with other value systems and also makes us more sensitive to transitoriness and temporary relevance. On the other hand, his œuvre represents the struggle of an artist from the 1980s and 1990s to create a complex artistic language in which the clear formal determinations with their latent expansionist potentialities are only relevant in close association with the cultural, anthropological context of the meaning of the form in which historical processes are embedded. This also implies that the virginal naïveté of future-oriented, evolutionist, and teleological utopias with external (quasi

I emigrated in 1973 to Israel. I left Argentina because the political situation was becoming unbearable, and because my students were increasingly in danger. I could feel that disaster was imminent.

I had a crisis there, of course, because nobody knew me or my work. So I taught and looked at paintings and pulled out their colors like a poet looking for words.

proaching his father's Andalus from seas of unstriated sand, yet I cannot sanction any of his remarks on the fallibility of the city-builders. Only when we are willfully directed through their boulevards and circumnavigate the relevant monuments will our

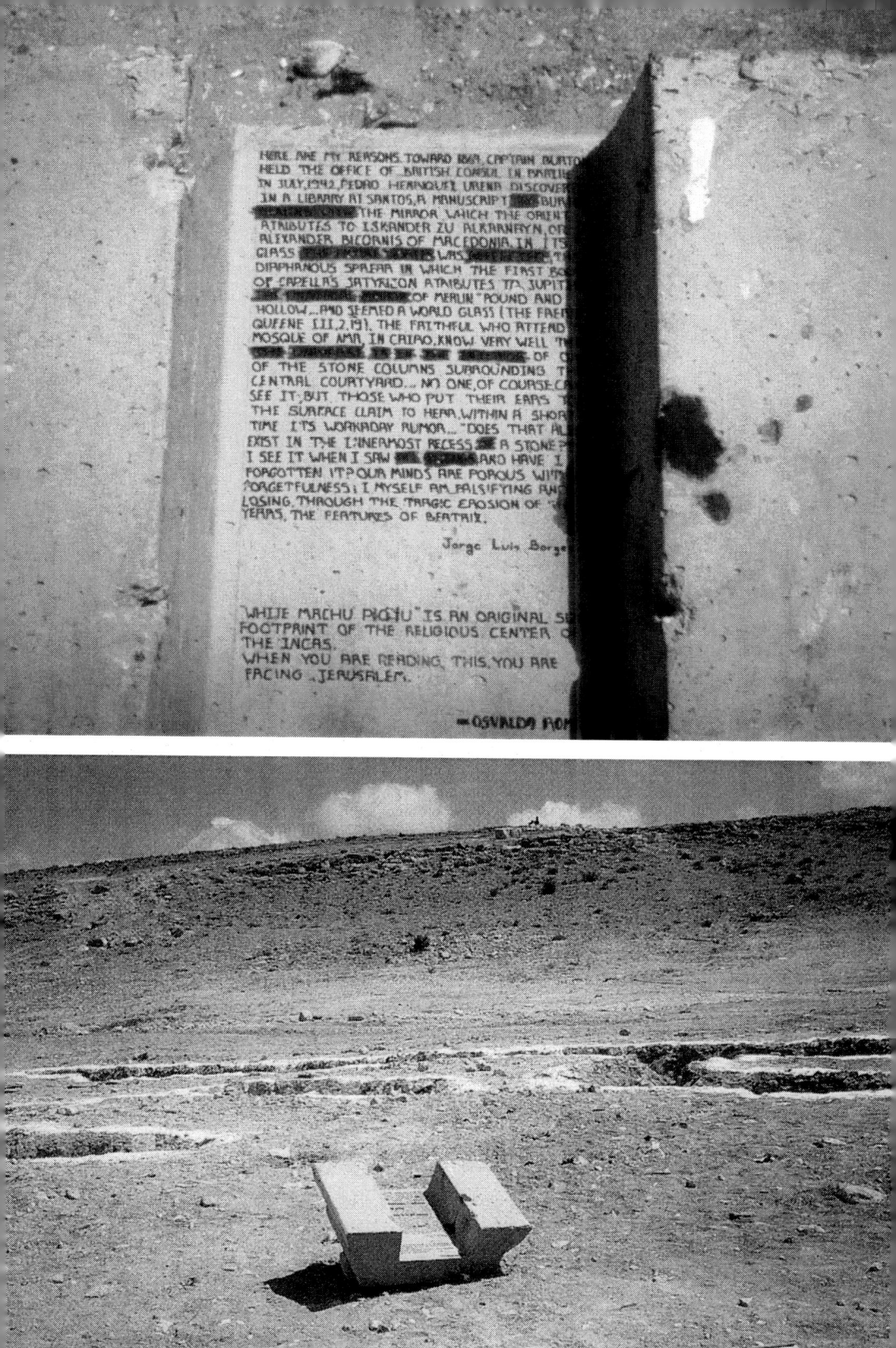

HERE ARE MY REASONS. TOWARD 1867, CAPTAIN BURTON
HELD THE OFFICE OF BRITISH CONSUL IN BRAZIL;
IN JULY,1942, PEDRO HENRIQUEZ UREÑA DISCOVERED
IN A LIBRARY AT SANTOS,A MANUSCRIPT ▓▓ BURTON
▓▓▓▓▓ CITES THE MIRROR WHICH THE ORIENT
ATRIBUTES TO ISKANDER ZU ALKARNAYN,OR
ALEXANDER BICORNIS OF MACEDONIA.IN ITS
GLASS ▓▓▓ ▓▓▓ ▓▓▓▓ WAS ▓▓▓▓▓▓ THE
DIAPHANOUS SPHERA IN WHICH THE FIRST BOOK
OF CAPELLA'S SATYRICON ATRIBUTES TO JUPITER
▓▓ ▓▓▓▓▓ ▓▓▓▓▓ OF MERLIN "ROUND AND
HOLLOW...AND SEEMED A WORLD GLASS (THE FAERIE
QUEENE III,2,19). THE FAITHFUL WHO ATTEND THE
MOSQUE OF AMR,IN CAIRO,KNOW VERY WELL THE
▓▓▓▓ ▓▓▓▓▓▓▓▓ ▓▓ ▓▓ ▓▓▓ ▓▓▓▓▓▓▓▓ OF ONE
OF THE STONE COLUMNS SURROUNDING THE
CENTRAL COURTYARD...NO ONE,OF COURSE,CAN
SEE IT;BUT THOSE WHO PUT THEIR EARS TO
THE SURFACE CLAIM TO HEAR,WITHIN A SHORT
TIME,ITS WORKADAY RUMOR..."DOES THAT ALL
EXIST IN THE INNERMOST RECESS OF A STONE?
I SEE IT WHEN I SAW ▓▓▓ ▓▓▓▓▓▓ AND HAVE I
FORGOTTEN IT?OUR MINDS ARE POROUS WITH
FORGETFULNESS;I MYSELF AM FALSIFYING AND
LOSING,THROUGH THE TRAGIC EROSION OF THE
YEARS, THE FEATURES OF BEATRIZ.

                    Jorge Luis Borges

"WHILE MACHU PICHU" IS AN ORIGINAL SI▓▓
FOOTPRINT OF THE RELIGIOUS CENTER OF
THE INCAS.
WHEN YOU ARE READING THIS,YOU ARE
FACING JERUSALEM.

                    —OSVALDO ROM▓

conquest approach anything like a totality. Mothers will no doubt continue to instruct their children to dream of new and variant futures, but I hold stubbornly that the ruins in which they slumber will dictate still the shape of their reverie.

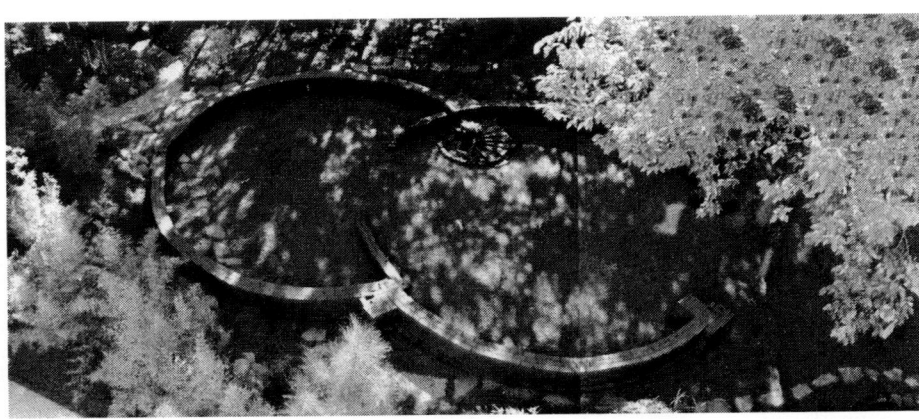

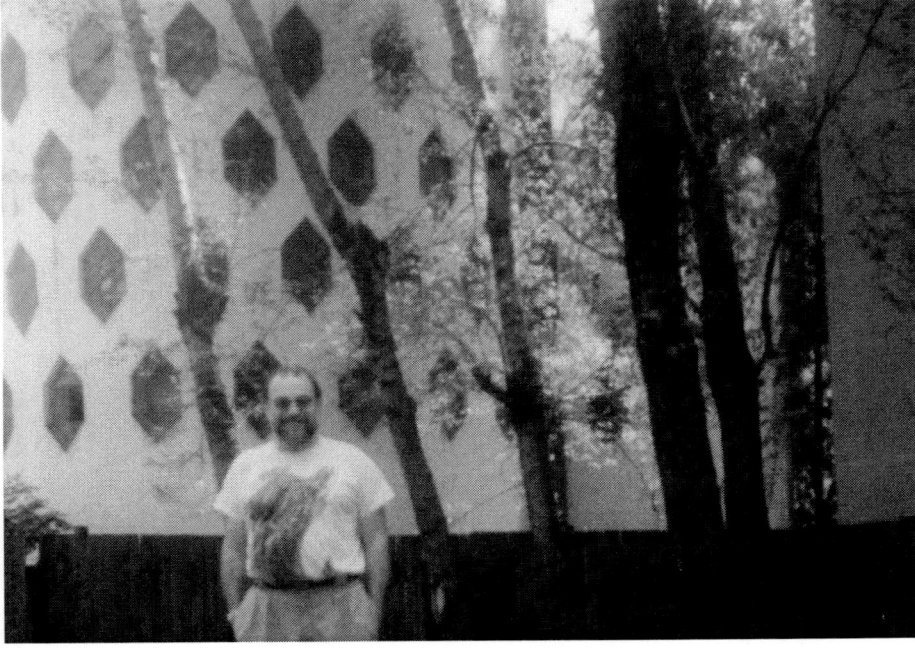

mythological) legitimization is seen here from its flip side, out of which the artist can draw reserves of still possible micro-utopias from the fragments of dismantled utopias, from the ruins of homogeneous value structures that are no longer tenable.

In Osvaldo Romberg's œuvre we see a surprisingly intimate link between cultural and historical formations and architectural structures, or fragments of visual three-dimensional design from a variety of epochs and cultures. It seems as if he were at home everywhere and at any time. His nomad-like existence is a permanent situation, not an experiment restricted to a certain territory or time period. The language which he has developed comprises public competencies as well as collective references to cultural history; at the same time, it incorporates his specific individual situation and uses it as a starting material for new personal concepts. These intimate situations are part of a common cultural history, while they also impact on the reading of this cultural history by perceiving the permanent flow of historical processes in the context of immediate, concrete, and anthropological realities, promoting authentic strategies of subversive micro-utopias.

In 1973 – 1974 when I looked at all of these color swatches on the wall with their numbers and text, I wondered why an exercise in painting could not be considered a work of painting itself? If Liechtenstein calls large format comics painting then why can't the very process of painting, through an organizational system like that of the Bauhaus or of the chromatic circle, be a painting?

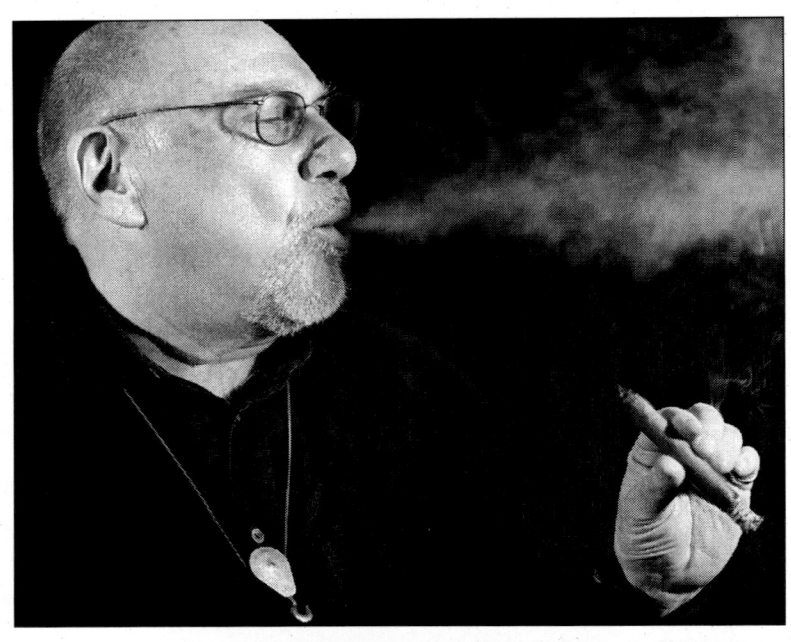

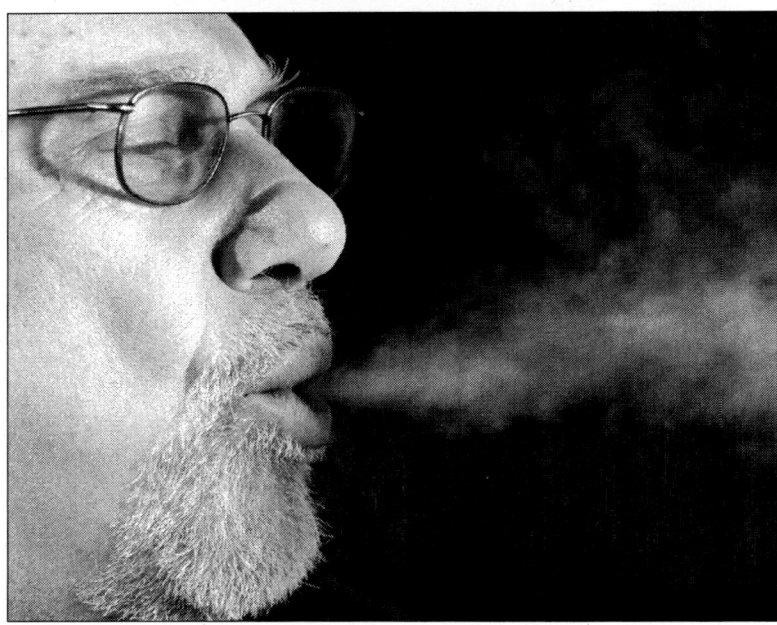

ABOUT
TRANSPARENCY

A traveling salesman running his wares up and down the American West Coast had the difficult task of selling unsuspecting homebodies *The Short History of Love, Doubt and Glory*. It came in three volumes. It is common knowledge that the economic viability of door-to-door products depends on a system of integrated

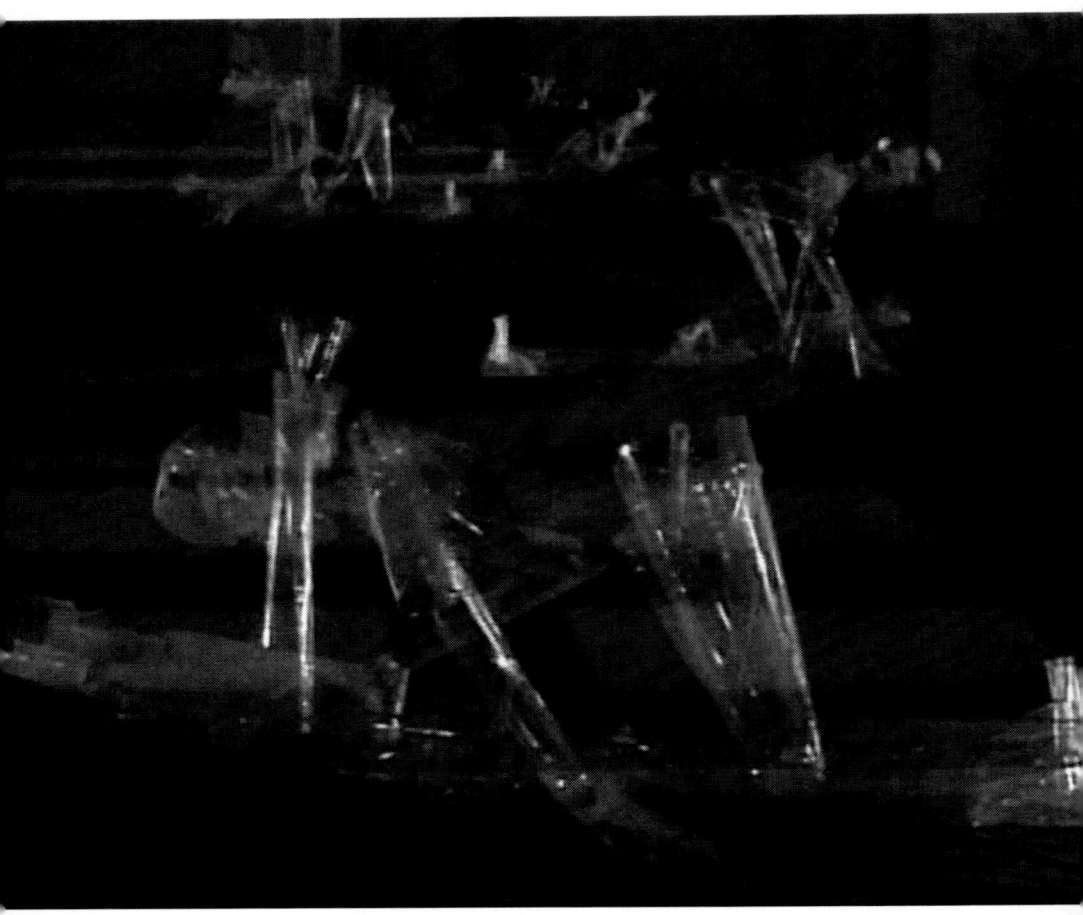

o.r., we will never forget anything
JEAN-MICHEL RABATÉ

Listening to Osvaldo Romberg's opera *Besame Mucho* for the second time, I was suddenly touched by a powerful affect coming from something that was not visual but musical: I heard with a distinctness never felt before the perfect enunciation of Edith Piaf singing, half-shouting and half-crooning the famous line: "Rien, rien de rien, je ne regrette rien..." In this almost archaic delivery and passionately rolled rs, an *r* which sounds like the continuation of an *or*... (said in French of course) I could catch, among other layers, a trace of my grandmother's tone of voice, of her long lost Berry accent. I was then reminded of Roland Barthes's disquisition on the "grain of the voice," of the wonderfully original if somewhat cranky opposition he establishes between Panzera and Fischer-Diskau. For Barthes, the "grain of the voice" is the revelation of the "materiality of the body" when it speaks its mother tongue. Here is for example how he praises Charles Panzera for his rs:

...Panzera carried his r's beyond the norms of the singer – without denying those norms. His r was of course rolled, as in every classic art of singing, but the roll had nothing peasant-like or Canadian about it; it was an artificial role, the paradoxical state of a letter-sound at once totally abstract (by its metallic brevity of vibration) and totally material (by its manifest deep-rootedness in the action of the throat.) This phonetics – am I alone in perceiving it? Am I hearing voices within the voice? But isn't the truth of the voice to be hallucinated? Isn't the entire space of the voice an infinite one?

installments. Still, our salesman had a hard time convincing his customers of the coherence of his merchandise in its three separate parts: a middle English bestiary, an ahistorical sitcom and a puppet show. The web behind these swollen elements of human histories and practices was anything but opaque. Worse yet, the man

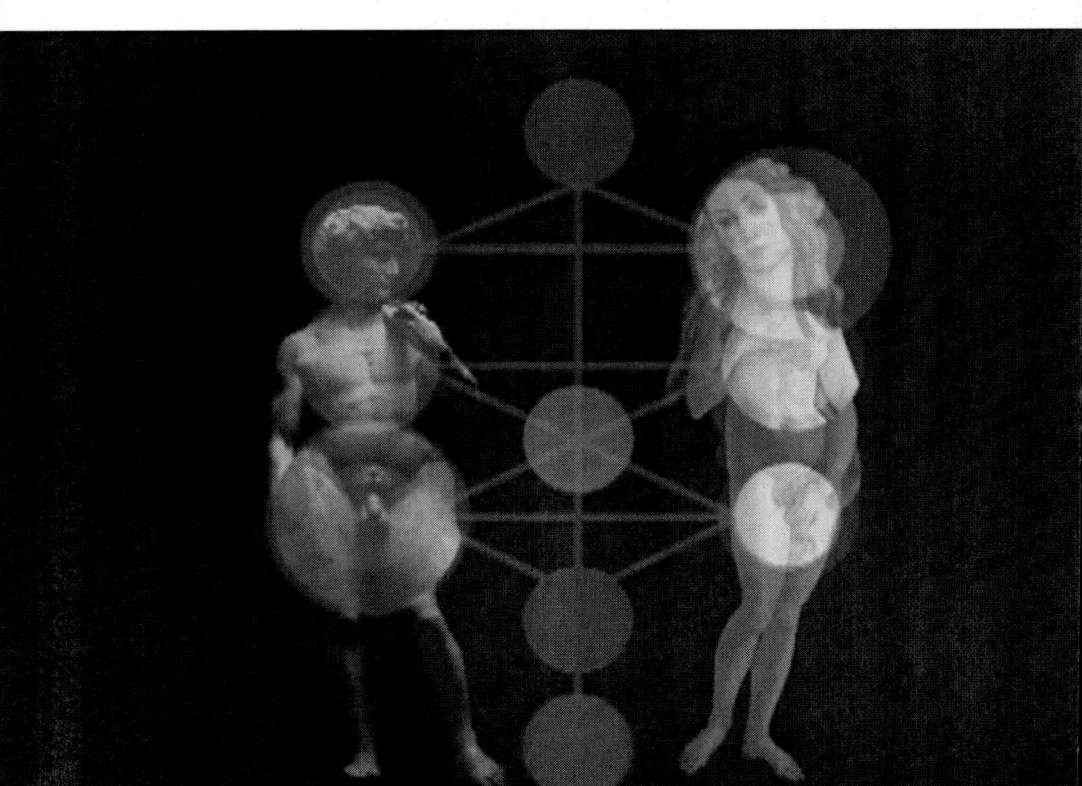

I can recapture Barthes's question ("Am I hearing voices within the voice?") and rephrase it in the context provided by Osvaldo Romberg's video: even though I know it is Edith Piaf who sings, I see the dangling and half-transparent mannequin, and have to suppose that it is from its throat that the sounds emerge. Its eerie transparency, a transparency akin to what art-critic Jeremy Gilbert-Rolfe has called the "technological sublime" sends me back to the materiality of my body, of my own voice. The sublime of a disembodied body made up of translucent plastic nevertheless contains the ghost of a voice whose materiality touches me to the heart.

Starting from this paradox, this tension, I would like to suggest that it applies broadly to Osvaldo Romberg's entire production, above all to his strategic hesitation – I should write his "OR" to pun, in a Barthesian mode, or his initials, already encrypted in the particular pronunciation of Rien as ORien – between two traditions that have dominated the twentieth century: that of high modernism which would take Picasso as an obvious hero, and that of postmodernism with Duchamp often seen as an intellectual and abstract antidote to the sexual romanticism that still lurks in much of

I really do prefer art of the Renaissance to the art of today – maybe I'm conservative.

I play with Renaissance images, the same ones that I admired as an adolescent, and after all these years of studying I can understand Rubens' relationship to his style, Leonardo's neuroses and his style. Michelangelo's all-consuming guilt over his sexual life and the way in which he sublimates the human body as melting into the tempest: the confusion of landscape and the being.

in question did not have the most pleasing demeanor, his sense of hospitality being somewhat skewed towards small talk, anxious flirtation and a twitch in his left eye. Indeed, this last irritation was perhaps the thing he communicated best of all. When his time in the West was spent along with his employer's generous stipend

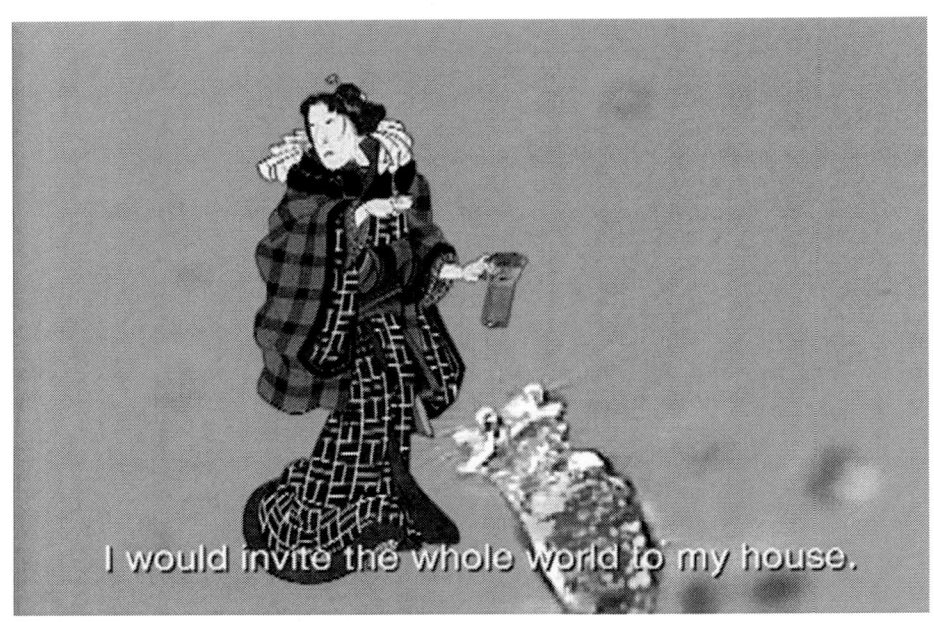

I would invite the whole world to my house.

Picasso's works. Picasso is clearly quoted in an epigraph that opens the opera, while Duchamp is probably behind the machine-like copulations that send us back to the endless interactions between the bachelors and their bride (even if this bride has chosen to live in a brothel).

Insofar as Romberg is post-Duchampian artist, one could think of Duchamp's momentary decision to retire not to a brothel but to Buenos Aires, just after the First World War. It seems that he did not take well to Buenos Aires, which he found small, provincial, and full of prejudice, but he nevertheless found enough mental peace to concentrate on chess playing. He left a deep impact at least in the person of Xul Solar, who later perpetuated the Duchampian spirit in Argentina. Just a little after Duchamp had returned to France by steamer, another Argentinean artist who was to leave a no less deep mark on the century, Jorge Luis Borges, would return from Europe. In March 1921, Borges and his family went home after a stay abroad of more than seven years.

Wondering whether I could situate Romberg either as a modernist or post-modernist, I came across a curious para-

I have been through many years of different therapies, and the greatest thing is that I am still alive. The greatest accomplishment of my life has been to stay healthy.

I do not think of psychoanalysis as healing, or fixing, but you can look to it as a tool, as a funnel. It is first introspection, then confession and lastly rendering neurosis productive. It corrects the place in which you put neuroses; that sometimes means putting them on a canvas.

and he returned home with nothing to say for himself, many eyebrows were raised. Had he not, after all, taken this particular commission upon himself? Had he not left behind mother and child for his fruitless coastal tour? Phone calls were made,

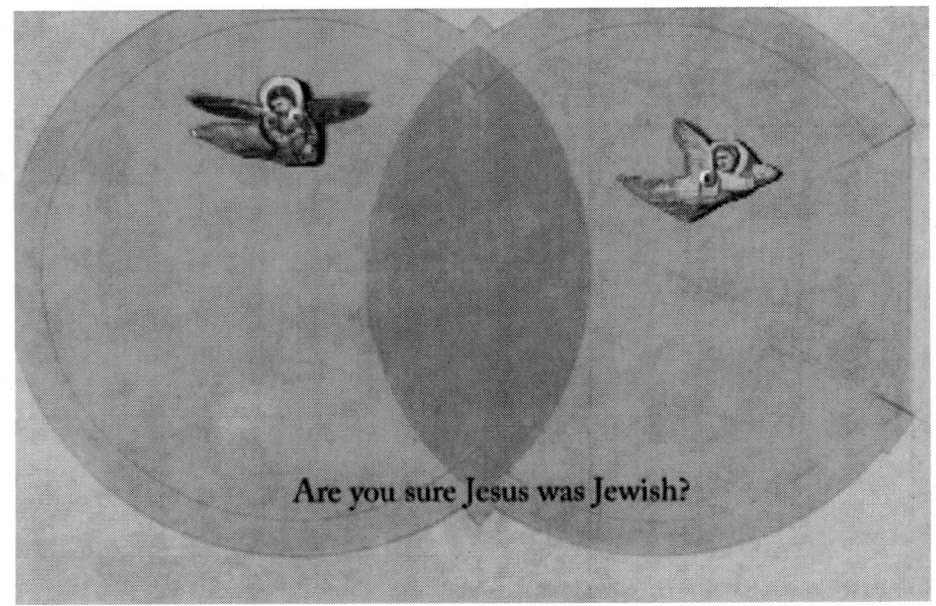

graph written by Borges in the Preface he composed specifically for the first volume of his collected works in French, in the prestigious Pléiade series of *Œuvres Complètes*. This is a text dated Geneva, 19 May 1986, therefore one of his last writings, and it carries clear words that nevertheless seam to conceal a posthumous riddle:

> This book is made up of other books. I am not sure whether a continuous reading is the best solution in this case, it might be more convenient to enter in and out at random as one leafs through the pages of an encyclopedia or of Burton's *Anatomy of Melancholia*.(…) Eliot wrote that it is less important to know what one wants than what the century wants. He claims this, as if drunk on universal history. Is it necessary for me to say that I am the least historical of men? The circumstances of history touch me like those of geography and politics, but I thing that as an individual I am above these seductions. 'A thing of beauty is a joyce forever,' John Keats wrote in a memorable way. In order to enjoy any work adequately, we have to situate it in its historical context. There are nevertheless,

Early psychoanalysis in the '60s was so fanatical. Psychoanalysis was very popular in Argentina, and so it influenced a lot of my work. Two of my early works were called "The Great Controller" and "My sisters, my mother and myself."

coworkers were questioned, books were cooked and superiors were incensed. Accusations flew like plates at a wedding. No specialists were called in for fear they might provide a counterproductive albeit illuminating exegesis. And then, in the dead

Jesus reappears in the psychoanalytic ambiance of Buenos Aires. Lacan and Freud interrogate him.

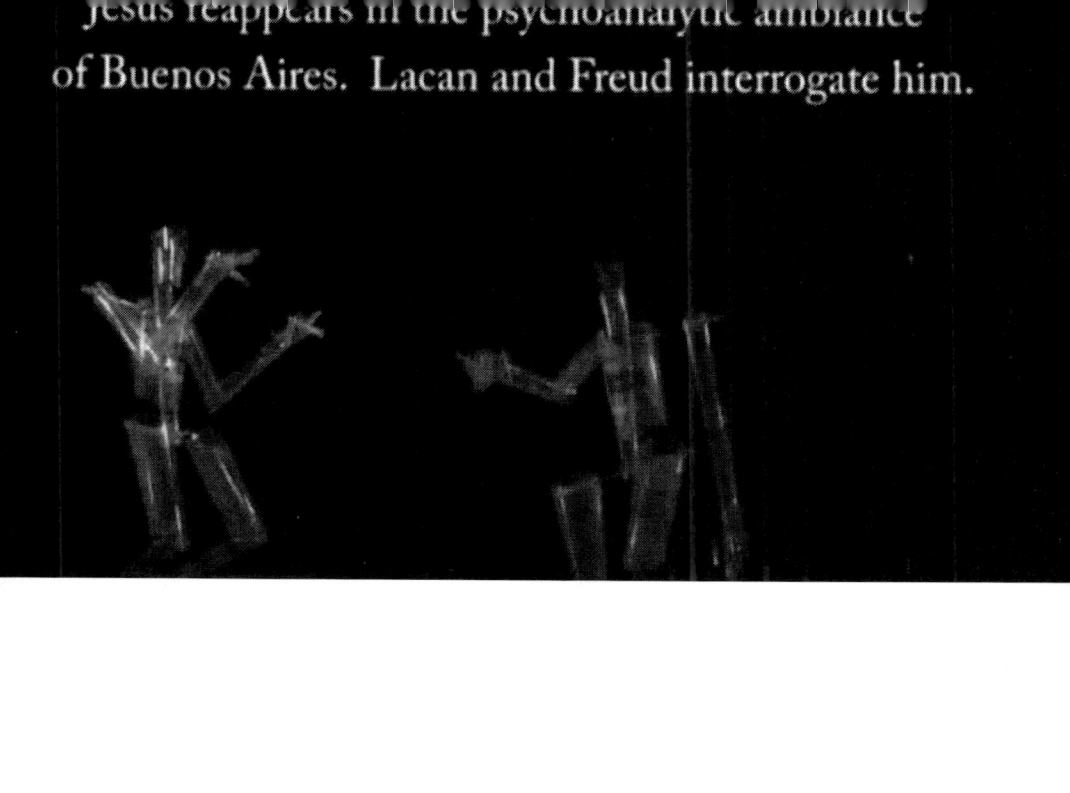

of one New English night, the news broke. He had left his home, teething son and seething mother behind and gone to the other side. Sightings true and false were reported daily. Gossip spread like sweetener at a board meeting. Clarity came when

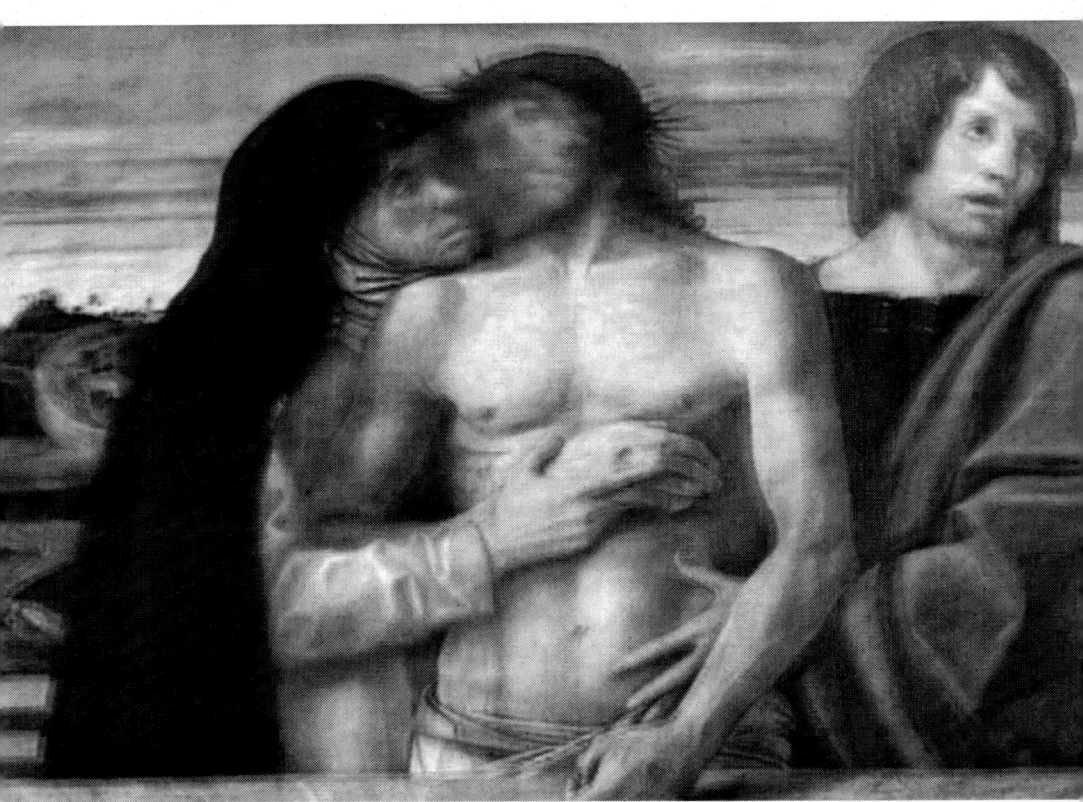

moments of happiness that are singular and eternal.

Why, in a preface which seems to attack Eliot's historical modernism (in the name of a Keatsian enjoyment of the atemporal eternity in the instant) is Joyce's name slipped almost invisibly, in such a cunning way that no editor of the Pléiade seems to have noticed it? One could imagine a footnote like: "Sic. Read joy instead of joyce. Borges may have wished to pay an ultimate albeit ironic homage to the Irish writer who has often inspired him." Of course, one will not find this note at the bottom of page x, in a Preface which names Coleridge, Wordsworth, Emily Dickinson, Flaubert, Hopkins, Browne, and Burton. In a tellingly symmetrical fashion, Joyce as the emperor of all puns sees his own name punned into Keat's "joy for ever," in a joke that is not above the level of a mischievous schoolboy's. One knows how ambivalent Borges was towards modernism (from Eliot to Pound and Joyce and Woolf) although a number of poems and essays praise the achievements of the Irish writer. It would be necessary to reread the fabulous tales devoted to Pierre Ménard, the French poet and essayist author of the Don Quichotte (1939) or to Funes, mister memory himself (1942) to reach a

In my latest film I try to mystify the idea of love, in the sense that people put it morally. I try to expose people to the dilemmas of love. I begin "Paradise to Paradise" with a sentence from Picasso that I think he stole: "Love doesn't exist, only the fact of love exists."

It is a parody of many things. All my movies are sarcastic. I don't know that they are movies, actually, so much as digital paintings.

an anonymous tip revealed that he had been sleeping with the company director's wife and that neither he nor his son bore any relation to the estranged mother. In an instant, what had long been taken for ambition and emotional inertia revealed itself

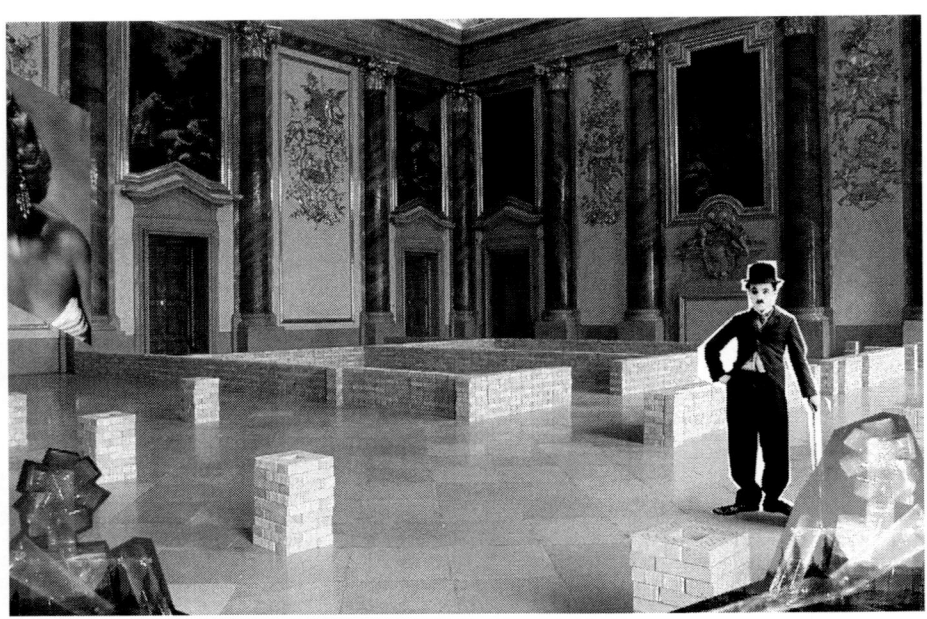

final assessment. Rather than comment on these well-known essays, I'd like to take my cue from earlier essays written by Borges while he was still threading his way within the Spanish and Argentinean avant-garde. I use the same French Pléiade volume to refer to these theses.

One essay in particular seems to me highly relevant in the context of Romberg's work. It is one of the so-called "Ultraist" manifestos written by Borges, and it opens the first issue of *Proa*, an Argentinean avant-garde review published in August 1922 (let us know that this is the year *Ulysses* and *The Wasteland* were published). In this rather vehement proclamation, Borges attacks relentlessly "The Futility of the Cult of the Ego," and debunks the "misprision" he sees in the concept of the ego. "I think I can prove that personality is a misprision caused by a presumption born out of habit without any metaphysical foundation or proper reality." Borges' essay keeps reiterating: "The ego does not exist" (five times).

Here is a typical exemplification:

> I, as I write, am only a certainty that is looking for the words which will be the most apt to gain your attention. This statement, as well as

People say my work is not art. Still, if you create commentaries on something and they are very sophisticated, then you can say that it is art. Roland Barthes said the future of literature is literary criticism. I believe that an author is an author, period. I do not work collectively but as a director of production: maybe it is my generation, but while I accept the ideas of other people I will still always follow my own obsessions.

to be a queer game of cuckolding Cluedo: "the Salesman in the boardroom with the impossible commission." Did he really think it would convince her to leave the cardboard-clad executive? Whatever the case, before the week was out, the scalded

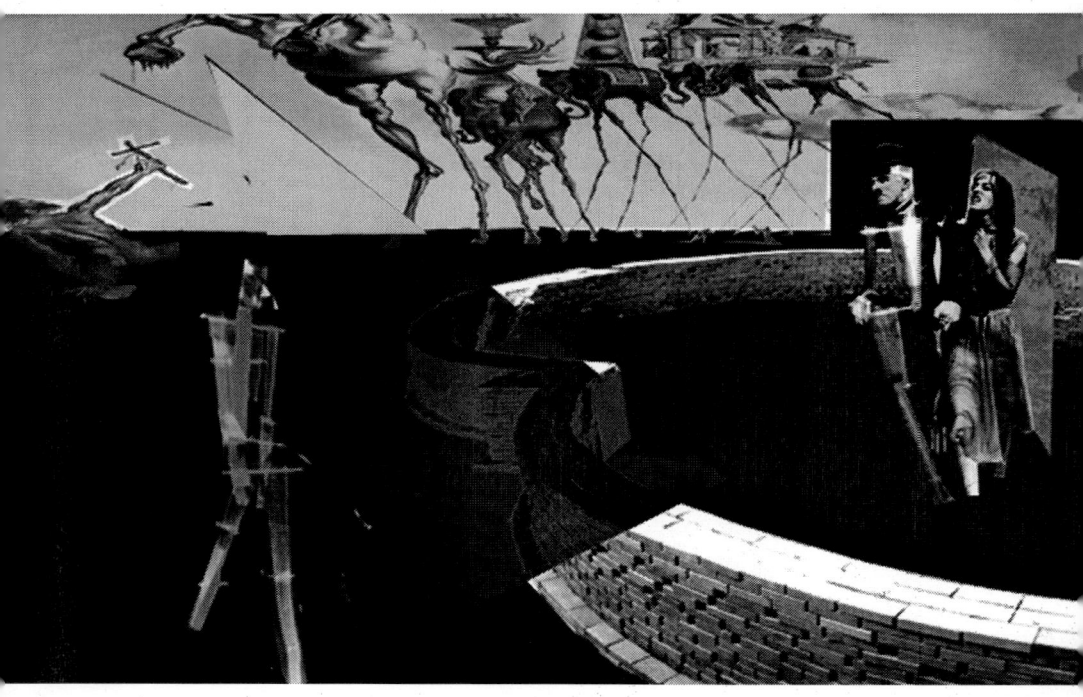

some muscular sensations and the vision of the blooming treetops facing my window constitute my current ego. It would be impertinent and unreasonable to suppose that in order for this psychic aggregate to enjoy a true validity, it would have to derive from an ego, from a hypothetical J.L.B related to Sevillian, Basque, and Navarrean origins, and particularly inclined to sophisms, puns and all sorts of verbal pyrotechnics.

One should evidently pay attention to differences in the historical contexts, and understand why Borges can attack modernismo in the name of an ultraismo he will later reject, while being so close to Eliot's thesis on impersonality that dominated Anglo-American modernism. What matters here is that I think I have found a theoretical basis and a local sensibility that fit with my general appreciation of Romberg's work: I see it as an attack on the illusions generated by the cult of the ego, while it glorifies creativity and intelligence, it produces the paradox of a selfless art of the self. This anti-egotism is the radical remedy to the widespread artistic narcissism that has flourised in the name of a post-modernist "anything goes" sensibility.

I have a double agenda, a family and my art. There is a fine line between them, and it is a complicated one to maintain. It is very difficult and demanding to be crazy enough in the studio to create fantasies and, a few minutes later, to work on reality, even though my family gives me enormous stability and love.

superior decided on revenge. Through a network of book peddlers and news dealers, the twitching off-sider was found and done away with, all attempts at escape and explanation ignored. That night, the boss slept soundly, in a devoted household and with a clean legacy.

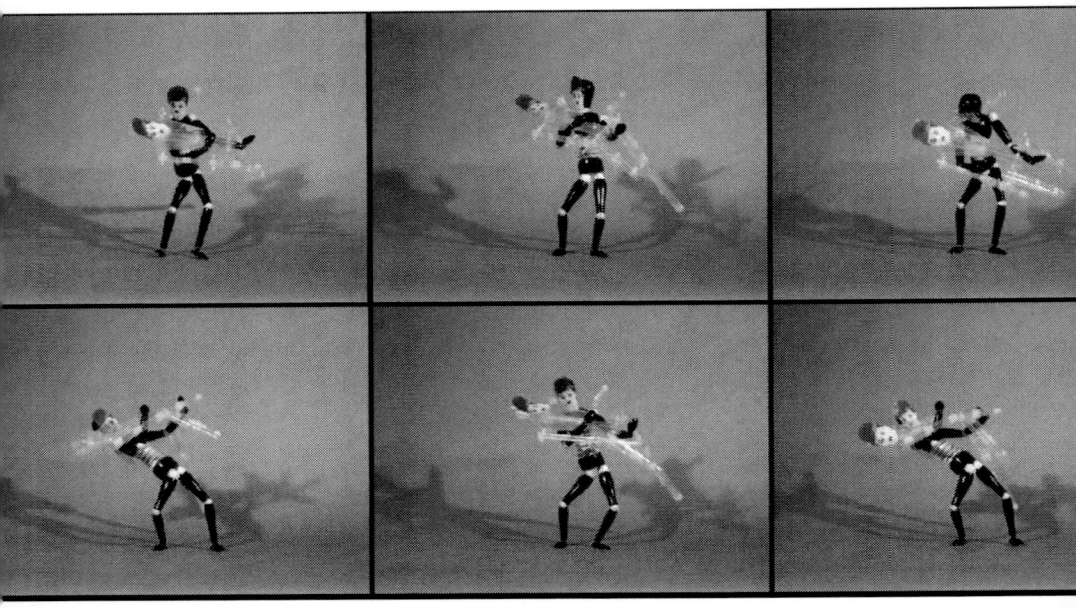

This leads me to a bolder global hypothesis about art today: it seems to me that the main issue is not so much about creativity (since everybody can be creative nowadays, and most people often are, with results that are not always entirely catastrophic) as the wish to reconcile creativity and critical intelligence. In short, today's crucial question would be: how can one overcome the anguish of a silence and sterility that has marked the French avant-garde from Mallarmé to Duchamp in the post-Bride years, without falling into Picasso's indulgent and self-mythologizing *débraillé*? How can one produce artworks that are both sensuous shapes still pleasant to the eye, while keeping in the mind the need to dissociate oneself from the pure mercantilism of capitalist markets?

Romberg's work has passed through quite a number of stages, from the more analytic moment of the famously didactic chromatic value tables presented as so many "explicitations" of famous paintings, to a more synthetic and architectonic moment with the modelizations of churches and sacred spaces, and its dynamism has not stopped. Without attempting to foresee where it will go as to expand and engage with our "post-medium" condition, to take up Krauss's

useful category, media artist like Marcel Broodthærs, I would simply like to pause and stress the subjective position that both enables and frames this type of work. It is in this selfless or egoless egotism of the work as work that I can become one not with the artist, not with the Romantic myth of the genius, who from Picasso to Pollock still seduces once in a while, but with the work as it presents itself in its simplicity, purity, and elegance. Then and only then can I "accompany" it, like for instance by humming once more, in a slightly lower scale: "Non…Rrien, rrien de rrien, je ne rregrette rrien… Ni le bien, ni le mal, Tout ca m'est bien egal! …Et demain je rrecommence a zero…"

*There is a mythology about looking at great painting. If I have
a perfect copy of the Holbein's Ambassadors then I don't care
where the original is, because it will have the same effect.*

*Once I was in the National Gallery in London, sitting for an hour
in front of the Ambassadors. Next to me, a man was almost
crying, and so was I. After a while I asked him who he was. He
was a scientist, and he said that he was moved because of the
way Holbein describes the scientific objects of the time. I cried
because of Holbein's vision of the world: the excellence with
which he depicts his era. Jesus Christ is on the left wall on a cross;
you have to be very precise to perceive that it is a fiction. There
is death on the floor, but of course you can only see it if you view
the painting from a corner. Otherwise, you don't see death, which
is very much a metaphor for the way we approach death. Then
there are all of the scientific objects in the middle: the picture
embodies a society. This is what is missing in modern art, and
what I hope is not missing in my work.*

I have four children, Joanna, Noa, David, and Victoria, each one of them different, each one of them wonderful for different reasons. My children are all involved with the arts, although I never pushed them in that direction. No matter what they will do, I will be happy so long as they are.

My wife, who is an extraordinary woman, is my companion of almost thirty years. She is the center and the axis of this beautiful interaction that is my life. I met Raquel in Israel almost thirty years ago. Her studies, teaching and writing on anthropology have greatly enriched our relationship: the meeting of our separate passions has been the source of inspiration for me. We are "compañeros" and together we have faced and overcome many difficult times. We enjoy being alone as a couple, which can sometimes last for months at our house on a solitary beach in Isla Grande in Brazil. Sometimes I think of us as being centaurs in the way that we integrate our different qualities.

FIGURES

FIGURES

ABOUT ARCHITECTURE

FIGURES

ABOUT TRANSPARENCY

FIGURES

1959 - 1969: Osvaldo Romberg begins his career with woodcuts, transitioning gradually to sculpture, and then to land art.

1969 - 1972: O.R begins his analyses with the *Landscape as Idea*, initiating the reconstruction of landscapes according to typologies of morphology, line and color.

1973: O.R begins the deconstruction of color in the art-historical canon, developing a phenomenology of color based on the chromatic circle. In this analysis, color is no longer a tool of figuration, but instead exists in the service of language.

1980: O.R. completes his deconstruction of the history of art with "From Prehistory to Manet, an emotional reconstruction of Art History."

1985: O.R initiates the *Paradigma Series*. Informed by the work of Thomas Kuhn, O.R. compresses multiple paradigms of western painting onto a single canvas. This synthesis is both literal and figurative, its intent being the creation of artistic "generics."

1986: O.R reconstructs monumental ancient structures in full scale. These works —called *Translocations*— penetrate and restructure contemporary spaces and their experience.

1997: O.R. starts work on the *Theater of Transparency*, a series of filmic works about Jesus, Renaissance literature, and the history of sex.

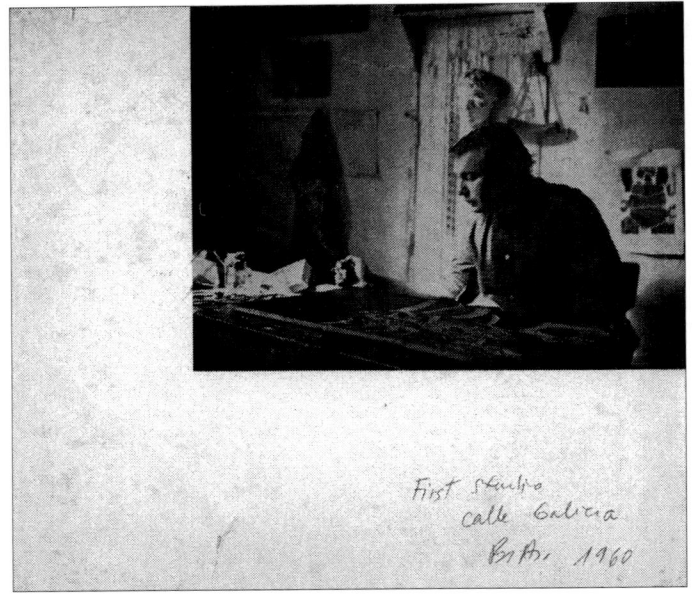

First studio
calle Galicia
Bs As, 1960

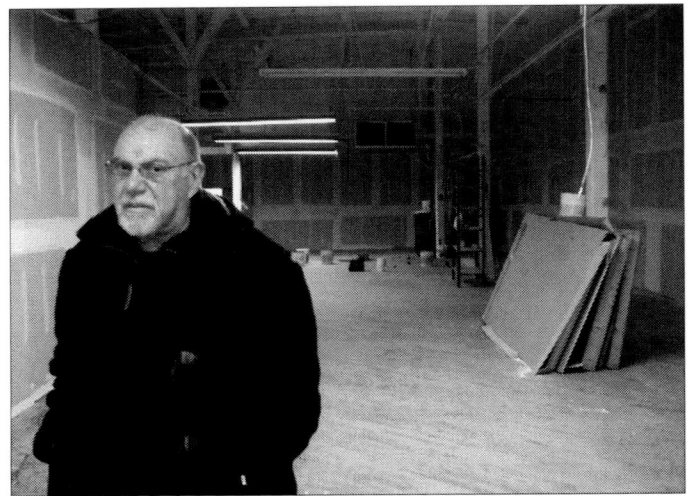

Top: First studio, Calle Galicia, Buenos Aires, 1960.
Bottom: Latest studio, Port Richmond, Philadelphia, 2008.